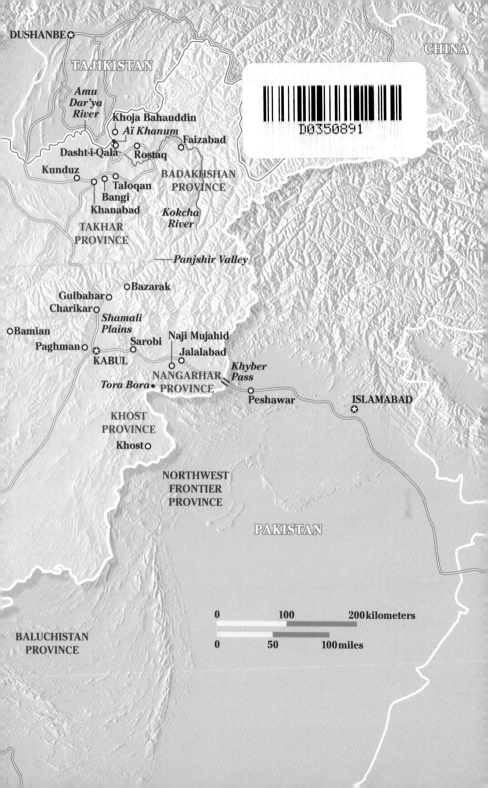

The Lion's Grave

Also by Jon Lee Anderson

Che Guevara: A Revolutionary Life
Guerrillas: Stories from the Insurgent World

THE LION'S GRAVE

Dispatches from Afghanistan

Jon Lee Anderson

Photographs by Thomas Dworzak

GROVE PRESS
New York

For Erica

"A Lion's Death," "The Warlord," "In the Court of the Pretender," "The Surrender," "City of Dreams," "Mullah Omar's Favorite Songs," and "The Assassins" appeared in slightly different form in *The New Yorker*.

Published simultaneously in Canada
Printed in the United States of America

FIRST EDITION

Library of Congress Cataloging-in-Publication Data
Anderson, Jon Lee.
    The lion's grave : dispatches from Afghanistan / Jon Lee Anderson.
      p. cm.
    ISBN 0-8021-1723-6
    1. Afghanistan—History—2001– 2. Anderson, Jon Lee. I. Title.
DS371.4 .A53 2002
958.104'6—dc21   2002070659

Design by Laura Hammond Hough

Grove Press
841 Broadway
New York, NY 10003

02   03   04   05   10   9   8   7   6   5   4   3   2   1

Foreword

Jon Lee Anderson was at his home in southern Spain on September 11, 2001, preparing to go to Sri Lanka to cover the civil war there for *The New Yorker*. He and his wife, Erica, and their three young children had lived in Spain since 1995, although Anderson was away much of the time, reporting and writing from Africa, Latin America, and the Middle East. He had recently spent several months working on a profile of President Hugo Chávez of Venezuela. The Andersons had decided to move to England for the coming school year, and Jon had stayed in Spain to tie up loose ends after the rest of the family left. He was about to join them to help with the unpacking before he flew to Sri Lanka to begin the new story.

His wife ended up handling the move to England pretty much by herself, since a few hours after the attack on the World Trade Center, Anderson was changing airline reservations and making arrangements for new visas. He was one of the first Western reporters to get into Afghanistan. The major newspapers and TV outlets have large staffs, and they rotated people in and out of the country, but *The New Yorker* didn't have anyone else on the ground. We kept

Anderson there for almost four months. He was in Afghanistan when the American bombing campaign began and he was still there when the new government moved into Kabul. He went home briefly, but was soon back in Afghanistan, covering the jockeying for power and the attempts to institute some sort of democratic, quasi-modern system on a premodern country.

Anderson is an experienced, intrepid journalist. He had spent time in Afghanistan in the late nineteen-eighties, when the mujahideen—the Afghan "holy warriors" who resisted the Soviet invasion of their country—were fighting against the Communist-backed government in Kabul. These mujahideen are one of several groups of fighters analyzed in his book *Guerrillas,* which was published in 1992. But a lot had changed since then in terms of how wars get covered. The biggest change was technological. Recently developed satellite phone systems had made it possible for reporters to call the office and file stories from pretty much anywhere. Some journalists who covered the war in Bosnia in the nineteen-nineties had sat phones, but the models available then were unwieldy and expensive. The sat phones used in Afghanistan at the end of 2001 looked like conventional cell phones and, when attached to a laptop, would transmit text and send and receive e-mail.

Without the new technology, it would not have been possible to cover the war in Afghanistan on a day-to-day basis. The country had fallen so far off the world map that it had lost its area code. There was pretty much no infrastructure: no electricity, no phone lines, no nothing. Batteries were charged with gasoline-powered generators, assuming you could get one. The equipment Anderson started out with was inadequate, and after filing two stories he reluctantly—and with some difficulty—returned to London for a few days to pick up a sat phone that would hold a signal long enough to transmit an eight-thousand-word piece. The keys on his laptop had begun to pop off and the screen had faded, so he also bought a computer that was designed to withstand frequent sandstorms. And he got his own portable generator—from a farm-supply store near his family's new house in the English countryside.

We established a method of working early on. I couldn't call him, because he couldn't waste the power needed to leave the sat phone on when he wasn't using it. So he called me every morning at around nine-thirty New York time and we exchanged information and made plans. But the bulk of our communication was done via e-mail, which is how he filed his reports and how we exchanged drafts. We decided to include some of the e-mails in this book because they illuminate a side of the war that we—intentionally— left out when the pieces were published in the magazine. The ones reprinted here are just a fragment of the hundreds of e-mails we exchanged, and we edited a bit for clarity. The narrator of *The New Yorker* stories is cooler than the narrator of the e-mails, who has to cope with frustrating logistical dilemmas and a good deal of old-fashioned danger.

—Sharon DeLano, senior editor, *The New Yorker*

The Lion's Grave

From: Jon Lee 9/11/2001
Sharon, I am guessing you never made it to the office. I hope every-one at the New Yorker is OK. I have to say that Sri Lanka seems very small, remote, and entirely irrelevant. I feel like I should be heading for Afghanistan, which I fully expect to be flattened any day now. Is the magazine planning any special coverage? Is there some-thing I can do to help?

From: Jon Lee 9/12/2001
I've reached my friend Peter, who is in Islamabad. He says that British Airways has cancelled flights to Pakistan but that the Emirates is still flying. As for visas from the Taliban to get into Afghanistan, this must be worked through their embassy in Islamabad. Peter says that journos, mostly TV crews, have already begun to swarm, but the Talib are being noncommittal and taking applications and telling people to come back in 15 days. He is working a connection inside the embassy whom he thinks is bribeable. (It might be possible to get a visa this way.) If the shit really hits the fan, of course, no visas would be needed. One can always find a way to get smuggled in, as I did before, during Najibullah's day.

There are two ways to proceed. One: forget going to Kabul and get into Northern Alliance territory through Tajikistan. (Wali Massoud, the brother of the wounded/dead? leader of the Northern Alliance, is their chargé d'affaires in London.) Or, two, take my chances with the Taliban out of Islamabad and then if that fails get myself up to the north.

If I want to keep my options open it would be good to get a second U.S. passport in London. The Talib won't like it if they see a Northern Alliance visa, and vice versa.

From: Jon Lee 9/12/2001
I've talked with Wali Massoud. He says "no problem" but that the Tajiks can drag their heels about visas. I guess he will wait until I am in London to spell things out more clearly. Says his brother is not dead, and recuperating.

From: Jon Lee 9/15/2001
Am now in England. Everybody is saying that Massoud died yesterday.

Ahmed Shah Massoud, 1952–2001

A Lion's Death

I met Wali Massoud a little over ten years ago, at a friend's house in Wimbledon. He was in his mid-twenties, a slight, amiable man with black hair and a mustache. Wali was the youngest son of an ethnic Tajik officer in the Afghan army and had come to Britain to study international relations. He had a famous older brother, Ahmed Shah Massoud, the Lion of Panjshir, who led a band of mujahideen that fought off seven major offensives by Soviet forces in the great mountain valley of Panjshir, in northern Afghanistan, during the nineteen-eighties. In 1992, three years after the Soviets withdrew from the country, Massoud's forces—the Jamiat-i-Islami (Society of Islam), a moderately conservative group composed mostly of ethnic Tajiks and led by the Islamic scholar Burhanuddin Rabbani—defeated the brutish regime the Soviets had left in power. Ahmed Shah Massoud became the defense minister and, later, vice president of the new Islamic State of Afghanistan.

In 1996, when the Taliban militia gained control of Kabul, the capital city, and most of the rest of the country, Massoud and Rabbani returned to the mountains in the north. With limited backing from Iran, Russia, and

India, they fought off the Taliban and managed to hold on to somewhere between five and twenty percent of the country. Massoud led a motley coalition of tribal-based guerrilla forces that are usually referred to as the Northern Alliance but are officially called the United Islamic Front for the Salvation of Afghanistan.

Wali Massoud stayed in London. He got married, had two daughters, and earned an M.A. in diplomacy. He is now the chargé d'affaires at the Afghan embassy to the Court of St. James's. The Northern Alliance controls Afghanistan's UN seat and all of its forty-odd embassies, except for the one in Pakistan, which is run by the Taliban. The Taliban is officially recognized only by Pakistan, the United Arab Emirates, and Osama bin Laden's homeland, Saudi Arabia.

The London embassy is a cream-colored early-Victorian building across the street from Hyde Park in Knightsbridge. I met Wali Massoud there at 11 A.M. on Friday, September 14, while Londoners were standing for three minutes of silence in memory of the victims of the attack on the World Trade Center. Wali, who is just as thin and amiable as he was a decade ago, wore a gray pin-striped double-breasted suit and held a cell phone, which rang again and again, and which Wali answered each time, with an apology to me. The previous Sunday, his brother had been attacked at his headquarters while giving an interview to two Arabs carrying Belgian passports. They were posing as television journalists and carrying a bomb. When it went off, it killed one of the "journalists" and one of Massoud's men and wounded Massoud and several other people. The second attacker tried to flee but was killed.

The suicide bombers had come into Northern Alliance territory from Taliban-controlled Afghanistan, across the front lines, which was an unusual breach of security and has thus far not been explained. "They arranged this with some-one at headquarters," a Northern Alliance official in London told me. "We are investigating." He said that the men are believed to have been either Moroccan or Algerian, and that they travelled from London to Pakistan before reaching Afghanistan. They are suspected of having links to an extremist group, the Islamic Observation Centre, in London.

Initial press reports said that Massoud had died in the attack, but all week Wali had been telling me that his brother was recovering. He was about to leave for Afghanistan, he said, to be with him. Wali was concerned about the stability of the coalition. Massoud was an extraordinarily gifted military tactician and was revered by his people. "The opposition can continue to function," Wali said, "but not the same as before." Then the phone rang again, and this time, as he listened, Wali hunched forward in his chair, holding his knees tightly together. He repeated the Farsi word *bale*—"yes"—and his voice became barely audible. He seemed about to weep.

Later that evening, the BBC confirmed Massoud's death. After the attack, he had been taken to a hospital in Tajikistan by helicopter. On Saturday, September 15th, his body was brought back to his hometown, the mountain village of Basarak, where he was buried. His thirteen-year-old son, Ahmed, spoke. "I want to be my father's successor," he said. While Massoud's bereaved relatives and thousands of followers were observing a period of mourning, the Taliban launched a large-scale military offensive against the Northern Alliance.

The timing and circumstances of the attack on Massoud, which came just two days before the strike on the United States, do not appear to be coincidental. Anyone who knew that the United States was going to be attacked and that Osama bin Laden and the Taliban would be blamed would also have known that Massoud would suddenly become an important ally for the West. "Without very good intelligence in Afghanistan, you can't do anything," an Afghan living in London said to me. "Bin Laden has a thousand caves to hide in." Ahmed Shah Massoud had been waging war in Afghanistan for more than twenty years, and he knew most of its hiding places.

From: Jon Lee 9/15/2001
With things so uncertain in the north, we may have to think of getting in through Pakistan after all. I hate joining a crowd, but, hopefully, I could find something of my own to report after some days on the ground. I gather that the Taliban are threatening Pakistan with war if they go along with the States, and are telling all foreigners to leave Afghanistan. That means no visas.

From: Jon Lee 9/16/2001
Re communications in Afghanistan. The only way is via sat phone. I found a place that sells them in London. Amazing little handheld things. 1,400 pounds including tax and charges of 4 quid a minute. Expensable?

From: Jon Lee 9/18/2001
Noushin, the woman at the Northern Alliance embassy, turns out to be an Iranian, an exile from the ayatollahs. It was crazy there, with phones ringing every few seconds. Anyone who has anything to do with Afghanistan is difficult to get to at the moment, as you can imagine. Noushin says that as soon as the period of mourning ends for Massoud, i.e., next Monday, she is confident that their people in Dushanbe will work to get me an entry visa for Tajikistan.

At her suggestion, I went to the Russian embassy, but got the run-around. I have one more route, a French NGO guy based in Dushanbe who has assisted journos in the past. I've sent him an e-mail asking for help in getting an invitation from the Tajik foreign ministry, whereupon the Russians will give me a visa.

Re my sat phone. I should have it tomorrow. It's an Iridium, which covers the planet, and the charges are significantly less than I was told. Only about two dollars a minute. Guess who's selling it to me? Arabs.

From: Jon Lee 9/19/2001
CNN's guy in Kandahar had to get out yesterday. That leaves only Herrigan (CNN), the CBC (Canadian) guy you mentioned, and the Daily Telegraph guy—all in northern Afghanistan.

From: Jon Lee 9/21/2001
The Tajik consul in Berlin says I can get a visa if I show up there first thing Monday morning. I will need a letter, faxed here today, requesting credentials to "cover events in the region." P.S. Around 4 P.M. my time I need to be with the sat phone technician so he can show me how to use it properly, and transmit data.

From: Jon Lee 9/23/2001
Thomas Dworzak [a German photographer assigned to cover Afghanistan for The New Yorker] has an assistant, Liza Faktor, in Moscow who has been liaising for us. She speaks English and seems very able. Thomas has a room for us to use as a base at the Hotel Avesto in Dushanbe.

From: Jon Lee 9/23/2001
Am in Berlin, with fingers crossed that I get the visa tomorrow morning. I heard via Liza Faktor in Moscow that Dworzak didn't get on today's chopper from Dushanbe to northern Afghanistan. Evidently

there is a big pileup of journos, and so far mostly TV people are getting in.

From: Jon Lee 9/24/2001
After all the anxiety, I have the Tajik visa: double entry and good for a month. They were very friendly and efficient.

From: Jon Lee 9/24/2001
Am in Munich. Talked to Liza Faktor, who says that Thomas Dworzak was unable, for the third time, to get on the chopper into northern Afghanistan. I will try to reach him a bit later. So far haven't been able to get a working line into Dushanbe.

From: Jon Lee 9/29/2001
Hi. Am now in a place called Rostaq, northwest of Faizabad, after a gut-wrenching seven-hour jeep ride. Came with an American guy who works for Shelter Now International, which builds homes and runs food-for-work programs for war-displaced civilians. He's the only American left in Afghanistan. He and all the other expats evacuated to Dushanbe after September 11, but he has returned. Dresses like an Afghan and speaks Farsi. He's a Christian, but not a Bible-thumper. He's connected, organizationally, to the German Christians who are locked up and pending trial by the Taliban in Kabul. Plan to visit the front line tomorrow, and also the village where Massoud was killed, where there is an interesting-sounding mujahideen commander, but also, reportedly, 200 reporters!!! Have e-mailed Liza to pass this news on to Thomas, so he knows where I am. He's still in the Panjshir valley, I think, but I hope he can make his way back up here.

From: Jon Lee 10/02/2001
I'm staying not far from the front, in a Shelter Now compound in Dasht-i-Qala, a town of about 50,000 people who live in brown-

colored adobe warrens that ramble over a stretch of desert ringed by mountains. There are two other reporters with me. Our compound has mud walls and mud floors and mud everything. We have several rooms, the floors of which are covered with large plastic sheets and cheap carpets. We sleep on pads that have been placed around the edges of the rooms. Outside, there is a large dirt patio with two hole-in-the-floor latrines, a vigilant mongrel dog, and—as of yesterday—a scorpion in the washroom, which has a barrel of water, a jug, and another hole in the floor. The house also has a generator, which means that we have light for several hours a day. This is a privilege, to say the least. There are probably only five generators in all of Dasht-i-Qala.

The refugees served by Shelter Now live in miserable shacks that spread across the land like litter, beginning just beyond the walls of our house. Tens of thousands of displaced people have arrived in Dasht-i-Qala. They live beside crude cemeteries—just mounds of earth decorated with poles and flags—and, here and there, Northern Alliance gun emplacements. There is dust everywhere, and the meandering tracks that serve as roads (less for cars than for donkeys, camels, and flocks of sheep and goats) are spongy with dirt that is powder-fine and that billows up in great, blinding spumes whenever a vehicle drives through it. The mujahideen race to and from the front in green Russian military jeeps, their windshields festooned with plastic flowers and pictures of the martyred Massoud.

It's not an easy work situation. Lots of people and yattering in the room, intermittent electricity, and field-radio conversations.

From: Jon Lee 10/04/2001
Thomas has arrived, and I saw Mamur Hassan, the local warlord, again. He is fine with me tagging along whenever possible. He was tired. Had not slept, for good reason. The Americans have told the Northern Alliance that as soon as Rumsfeld's trip is over, they are

going to begin massive air strikes. The Northern Alliance and, according to Mamur, secret allies among the Taliban, will begin a major offensive. They have promised not to fight among themselves and not to make reprisals against Taliban troops. He says that American ground troops will be involved in seizing airports and bin Laden bases. He was tremendously excited.

Yesterday, on the road outside Dasht-i-Qala, I was passed by a mujahideen driving a jeep with a blond man in the passenger's seat. He was obviously European or American, very pale, with short-cropped hair and glasses. He wore a camouflage outfit. I mentioned this to Mamur Hassan and asked him if the man was a Western military adviser. Mamur said that I must be mistaken. There were only Afghans in the car.

The boys in the radio transmission room in Mamur's house were engrossed in a little news bulletin that some of Mamur's people run off every week on a couple of computers and a printer. It is printed in Farsi. The boys told me that it had news about the front line, sometimes a poem, and currency rates for the Afghani and the dollar. Yesterday's issue said that the dollar had dropped significantly. This is, supposedly, because of all the journalists who are prowling around, putting money into Afghans' pockets. But also because of confidence that the Taliban are about to be defeated.

It is late, and I am running out of power.

From: Jon Lee 10/07/2001
Thomas was up late trying to send the photos via my sat phone. This is a problem. It takes about forty minutes to transmit and my system won't hold a signal for that long. There is another system that is better. Since we don't have it, Thomas will have no choice but to beg other media in the area, which leaves us somewhat dependent.

I have new material from Mamur on bin Laden, etc. He seems to blame it all on whacko Pakistani madrasah teachers and Arabs, whom he calls a bunch of pederasts.

I have rented a horse for the week.

From: Jon Lee 10/07/2001
It seems as though things are starting. We are told that Bush has spoken to the nation and that air strikes have hit Kabul, Kandahar, and Kunduz, and maybe other places. I hear some booms in the distance, whether bombing or shelling from the front line I don't know. The radio is hard to hear. Lots of static, and the sat phone seems to be clogged, but I will try to get this to you anyway. Mamur told me that sat phone communications would be jammed when the bombing started and that only the military satellites would be functioning.

From: Jon Lee 10/10/2001
Another big dust storm today, and a cold front. Visibility is almost nil, and the sat phone transmission is very bad. I've been trying for several hours to download two e-mails that are in my system. I am assuming one is the draft of the piece from you. I will keep trying.

I saw the commander again this morning. He was gracious and warm as always, but in a rush. A lot of mujahideen officers were there, and he was in meetings. Re the war, things are the same as yesterday. I've heard there is no fighting around Mazar today either, because of the dust. This may affect air strikes.

From: Jon Lee 10/12/2001
Am sending this to you from the summit of Aï Khanum. Beautiful day here. There was an unusually prolonged exchange of tank and rocketry this morning, but it has died down. Here's the new material.

The Warlord

A few days before the American and British air strikes in
Afghanistan began, I visited a man who is being held
prisoner in a hole in the desert. The hole is near Dasht-i-Qala,
a northern Afghan town a few miles from the Tajikistan border, not far from a hogback ridge of dusty hills that the
Taliban have, for some time, been trying to wrest from their
main opponents, the Northern Alliance. The Taliban and the
Northern Alliance fighters had come to within three hundred
yards of one another in places, and on the exposed ridges,
where the powdery earth was a grim geometry of sandbagged dugouts and trenches, they traded shots with sniper
rifles and heavy machine guns, while their rearguard positions lobbed tank shells back and forth.

The prisoner, a Taliban fighter who says his name is
Bashir, had been in the hole for about a month, since the
night he was caught by the Northern Alliance mujahideen
wandering around on his own in no-man's-land. His hole-
prison is ten feet deep and three feet wide, and it is covered most of the time by a piece of heavy metal tread from
a Russian tank. At the bottom, the hole turns into a cavity
that, according to his captors, is a comfortable six feet by

six feet. When Bashir is brought up to ground level, he has to climb a wooden ladder. This is a not an easy thing to do, because he also wears leg irons.

On the day I met Bashir, or, rather, observed him— for he was in a trancelike state of detachment—his leg irons had been removed. He was forced to walk over to where I stood, but he appeared to be weak, and he soon squatted down against a mud wall. He is about thirty, very thin, with a black goatee and short-cropped black hair. He wore a filthy green smock and his skin was smeared with dirt. His arms were tattooed with green dots, and there was a string around his neck from which hung a little purple book containing verses from the Koran. He was barefoot. His captors said that he has needle tracks on his arms, although I didn't see them. I did see a scar from a bullet hole on his right collarbone.

A group of mujahideen guards and curious children gathered to watch. Despite promptings from Mullah Omar, the warlord who is holding Bashir and wants to exchange him for five of his own soldiers who are being held prisoner by the Taliban, he didn't say very much—just his name, and that he is from Kandahar, more than four hundred miles to the southwest, where the Taliban have their headquarters. (And where the better-known Mullah Omar, the head of the Taliban, lives. Many Afghans use only one name, which can be confusing to Westerners.) "All the Kandaharis are like this," Mullah Omar said to me. "They never talk." They were not to be trusted, he said, which was why Bashir had to be kept in a hole. Mullah Omar is a slight, thirty-five-year-old man of Tajik ancestry. He said that the Taliban had offered him only three of his soldiers in exchange for Bashir, and that he and they were haggling about this over their field radios. I asked him why Bashir kept spitting, and he said it was because he was suffering from drug withdrawal. Some of what he had been spitting appeared to be brown, though. Was it blood? Had Bashir been beaten? "No, no," Mullah Omar reassured me. "We give him bread, milk—everything he wants. But we don't give him *charas*"—hashish, or opium. "He asks for it every day."

After a few minutes, Bashir was taken back to the hole, and Mullah Omar led me inside his compound to meet his sons. He assembled two groups of boys, all barefoot. One of the groups consisted of his ten sons, aged one month to twelve years, including a set of identical twins. The other group was made up of the five sons of his own twin brother, who was killed a few months ago by the Taliban. A few months before that, their eldest brother, Qari Kamir Alem, a relatively famous mujahideen commander, had been murdered. Mullah Omar captured six men who he said had betrayed Qari Kamir Alem and were responsible for his death, and he had them hanged. He had inherited his brother's command on the front line, and he claimed to have two thousand fighters, but this was almost certainly an exaggeration. He told me that he had begun fighting in 1979, when he was twelve years old and the Soviets invaded Afghanistan. As for his title of "mullah," he said that he had earned it by studying the Koran and other holy books in his home village—which is in the Khoja-i-Gar district, and is now occupied by the Taliban—and then at a madrasah in Pakistan. I left Mullah Omar as dusk approached and he and his men prepared for the sunset prayers.

The day after the air strikes began, I drove past Mullah Omar's compound, again at sunset, and looked out at the desert, toward Bashir's hole. His guards had brought their captive up for air, and he was standing in a shallow ditch they had dug for him. He was visible only from the torso up. He appeared to be rooted in place, half swallowed by the earth.

DASHT-I-QALA IS IN TAKHAR PROVINCE, and until last year the provincial capital, Taloqan, was the main base of operations for Ahmed Shah Massoud and the Northern Alliance. But Taloqan fell in heavy fighting, and Massoud retreated to a village closer to the Tajik border, about twenty-five miles northeast of Dasht-i-Qala. He was there on September 9th, when the two Arab suicide bombers, posing as journalists, set off a bomb while they were interviewing him. By then, the hills above Dasht-i-Qala were the last barrier between the Taliban and the border that provided the Northern Alliance with access to the outside world and supplies.

Dasht-i-Qala is near the confluence of two rivers—the Amu Dar'ya, which forms the border with Tajikistan, and the Kokcha, which runs into the Amu Dar'ya. The local Northern Alliance organization is called the Kokcha Union and is led by four commanders, each of whom represents a population center. They cooperate with the central Northern Alliance organization, which is nominally headed by Burhanuddin Rabbani, the president of the government formed by the mujahideen who took power in Kabul in 1992, when the Soviet-backed government fell.

The local commanders in the Northern Alliance negotiate with Rabbani's government for funds for their troops, but they have a great deal of autonomous authority in their districts. If an NGO wishes to build a school or an irrigation system or organize a food-for-work road-improvement project, it must make arrangements through the local commanders, whose bargaining power vis-à-vis the Northern

Alliance as a whole derives from the fact that they have small armies of their own. The commanders supply troops in the war against the Taliban and coordinate their activities along the front with the Northern Alliance defense minister—formerly Ahmed Shah Massoud and now General Muhammad Fahim, who took Massoud's place after the assassination.

The commanders within a district have a rotating system of leadership. Last winter, the Dasht-i-Qala commander, Mamur Hassan, led the Kokcha Union troops for a four-month period and then relinquished his duties to one of the other district commanders. Hassan is a landowner, and his men are extremely deferential to him, as if he were a feudal lord. He says that he has been at war, more or less constantly, for the past twenty-four years. He is of Uzbek heritage, and he studied at an American-built high school in the province of Helmand, in southern Afghanistan, and at Kabul's agricultural university, but he came back home to Dasht-i-Qala to work on irrigation projects. Then the Soviets invaded. He laughed when I asked what he would do after the coming war. "I will farm," he said. "I have three hundred *jeribs*"—a hundred and fifty acres—"of land. I can be a rich man." For the time being, he supplies trucks to his nephews, who work the farm and split the harvest of wheat, corn, melons, and lentils with him.

Mamur Hassan is a small, sturdy-looking man, and light on his feet. He has a beard of medium length that is mostly gray, and short-cropped black hair running to gray as well. He usually wears a long-tailed tunic and matching pantaloon outfit—which is what most Pakistani and Afghan men wear—and, over it, a military-style multipocketed vest. He has a wide nose, and large brown eyes with crow's-feet at the corners. He listens attentively and speaks with a warm, reedy voice, full of inflection, in Uzbek or Dari, the Afghan variant of Farsi. Mamur Hassan appears to be in his late fifties. Like a lot of Afghans, he does not seem to have thought much about his age, and when we first met he told me that his father, who he said was a hundred and seven when he died two years ago, was thirty when he was born. I pointed out that if that was the case Mamur Hassan would be close to seventy. He hesitated and began counting on his fingers. He said that he was born in the Muslim year 1322—1943 in the Christian calendar—and, since it was now 1380, he agreed that it was possible that he was fifty-seven or fifty-eight.

Hassan lives with his two wives and five of his seven children in a brick-and-concrete house surrounded by orchards, at the end of a dirt drive that passes through a small glade of trees running from Dasht-i-Qala to the Kokcha River. The town itself is little more than a rambling spread of walled family compounds set around an intersection of dirt tracks fronted by little shops with wooden shutters, many of them made from ammunition boxes. On the other side of the river is the front line. Hassan's house is small but comfortable and modern by local standards. The garden is lush—because it is irrigated—with a green lawn and a large plane tree. There is a raised concrete area in a corner for afternoon prayers and for sleeping outdoors in the hot summers. Pink petunias and red and white roses grow next to a concrete bungalow that functions as his staff headquarters and guest house. It has a carpeted room that is used for meals and meetings and prayers, a radio room, a kitchen, and a sleeping room. Large white geese wander along the dirt path outside, near a muddy stream. Two pens house a number of pheasants, which occasionally break out in a peculiar song, a staccato clatter that ranges briefly through several tempos and then stops abruptly. There is an antiaircraft battery on one side of the house.

The first time I visited Hassan, he sat in a chair about twelve feet away from the one that had been placed on the lawn for me. He raised his arm in the direction of a soldier standing twenty feet behind him, and called for his worry beads. An aide came running with a set of amber beads, which Hassan began working with his left hand. I noticed that when he put the beads down his hands trembled. From time to time, he took out a small round tin case of *naswar,* the tobacco-spice-herb mixture—a mild stimulant—that many Afghan men are addicted to, and tapped a little onto his hand, then popped it into the gap between his teeth and his lower lip. Two bodyguards paced around us, and when I reached into my bag for a notepad they looked especially alert. Later, after I had spent some time at the compound, they laughed and said that they thought I would understand their nervousness about journalists, since the men who killed Massoud had passed themselves off as reporters in search of an interview. When they were no longer suspicious, they greeted me with thermoses of tea and dishes of almonds and candies and tried out English phrases on me. Hassan invited me to stay at the compound when the air strikes became imminent.

It is not the custom in Afghanistan to invite guests into one's living quarters, since wives are not supposed to be seen. I never met the women in Hassan's household, but Hassan's youngest son, Babur Shah, a three-year-old toddler, played around our feet while we talked. Hassan occasionally called out to the little boy, remonstrating with him gently, but for the most part he just looked at him fondly. Babur Shah's older brother Ataullah, who is twenty, was also usually present, and took care of him. Ata, as he is called, has just received a scholarship to study journalism in China. Hassan has two other sons who live and study in Tehran, where one of his wives has a house. Hassan didn't want to send his sons away, but Ahmed Shah Massoud advised him to, so that he would not be distracted by having to look after them while fighting a war. He sent them to Iran because he could not afford to send them to Europe.

Mamur Hassan said that he was one of only two men still alive among the thirty from Dasht-i-Qala who took up arms as mujahideen against the Soviets in 1979. They had started out on their own, without any affiliations, he said, but later on, when Afghan Muslim leaders began receiving arms and funding from Pakistan, Saudi Arabia, and the United States, they threw in their lot with Gulbuddin Hekmatyar, the radical leader of an ethnic Pashtun mujahideen group. Hekmatyar was Massoud's rival. "At first, I was a member of Hekmatyar's party, and I fought against the Soviets but also against other Afghans," Hassan said. "We killed a lot of people and destroyed many places, and I regret this. I tell my sons not to have anything to do with political parties." He finally broke with Hekmatyar and joined Massoud, who offered to make a place for him when the mujahideen formed a government in Kabul in 1992. Hassan chose to return to Dasht-i-Qala instead. Now he helps out the Northern Alliance but maintains his independence. "I control a lot of men and a large area," he said. I asked whether the men he commanded owed their loyalties to him or to the Alliance, and he said, "To *me*."

There are apparently around five thousand soldiers in the Kokcha Union, with maybe a thousand in Dasht-i-Qala. "They are ready to fight for me whenever I order them to," Hassan said. The Alliance gave him two hundred

Kalashnikovs, and he regularly receives food for six hundred soldiers, but he makes up the shortfalls and provides everything else that is needed, like clothing and medicine. "I pay for it myself," he told me, "out of my own pocket." He laughed. "My family was rich, but we spent it all in the jihad"—the war against the Soviets in the nineteen-eighties and then for four years against the Afghan Communist government.

I asked Hassan what Islamic state he admired, or could see as a model for Afghanistan, and he said that Islam, as he understood it, was a civilized religion and allowed for states in which, for example, Muslims and Christians could live together without problems: "This is the kind of Islamic state we want." He cited Egypt and Saudi Arabia as two nations that he thought had managed to balance the Muslim faith while retaining basic freedoms and also bringing modernization to their countries. I asked what he felt toward unbelievers. "I don't think anything," he said. "I don't mind what they are." I thought that perhaps he was telling me what he thought I wanted to hear, but Hassan does seem to enjoy a reputation locally for moderation and fairness. "He's not all that worked up about religion," Shahmurat, a hulking farmer who has known Hassan for most of his life, said to me. "He's a democrat." Massoud Aziz, an engineer who lives in Dasht-i-Qala, said that Hassan is highly regarded, especially by the middle-class intelligentsia. "He has evolved since his early mujahideen days," Aziz said. "He was not a democratic man then, but he is now."

ONE MORNING, MAMUR HASSAN took me with him on an inspection tour of the front line. He sat next to the driver of his

*Mamur Hassan inspecting his troops on a hill overlooking the Amu Dar'ya
River and Aï Khanum, the site of an ancient city.*

Russian UAZ jeep and I sat between two of his bodyguards in the back seat. Two more bodyguards were squeezed into the space behind us. We drove up a huge dirty-yellow hill that housed a labyrinth of bunkers, dugouts, sandbagged bivouacs with howitzers, and Russian T-55 tanks disguised with straw matting, their cannons pointing toward the Taliban positions, which were barely visible through clouds of dust. We sped from bivouac to bivouac, and Hassan popped out of the jeep at each stop, dressed in a powder-blue tunic and green army fatigue jacket, a white skullcap on his head. He poked around the soldiers' dugouts and asked them what they had and what they needed, and jotted down what they told him on a pad. I went with him into an underground bunker with bare floors and Kalashnikovs and ammo clips hanging on the walls. "Only two blankets for ten men," Hassan noted. "My mujahideen are in bad shape."

The hill where Hassan's men were dug in overlooks the Amu Dar'ya, near where the Kokcha meets it. The flat plain between the hill and the river was honeycombed with large holes, and I realized later that this was what was left of the archaeological excavation site of Aï Khanum, where a great Hellenistic city flourished from the fourth to the second centuries B.C. The city had been surrounded by brick ramparts, with a monumental gate and several square towers. It was a formidable citadel with a palace, mansions, a theatre, a temple, and an arsenal. There has been widespread looting of antiquities in Afghanistan, not to mention the destruction of ancient sites by bombs and religious zealots. Many of the treasures from Aï Khanum were displayed in the Kabul Museum, which was vandalized, its collections dispersed in bazaars and on the illicit art market. The pockmarked plain I saw had apparently been bulldozed to facilitate the looting. The site is one of the main transit points for supplies and equipment coming into Northern Alliance territory from Tajikistan, and we watched people landing on the Afghan side of the river in what looked like a rubber raft. Trucks and other heavy items are brought across by barge. One of the bases of the Russian border guards who are still in charge of security in Tajikistan was visible on a craggy promontory on the far side of the river.

Around four o'clock that day, when the sun was already beginning to descend, I found Mamur Hassan at prayers with some of his commanders in his garden. When they were finished, he called me over and said, in a hushed, edgy voice, that the Americans were supposed to have begun bombing at 2 P.M. that day, but, because there was a sandstorm and poor visibility, they hadn't. "Maybe they have already begun bombing Kandahar or Kabul, or will tonight," he said. The Alliance's frontline units had been ordered to cease shelling, he explained, so that they wouldn't be mistaken for Taliban positions and get bombed. Driving back to the compound where I had been living, thirty minutes or so from Hassan's home, I heard explosions in the distance. They didn't sound like the usual howitzers or rockets. I turned around and returned to Hassan's base, to stay there for the night.

Mamur Hassan inherited his position in Dasht-i-Qala. He said that his grandfather owned a lot of livestock, and that his father made the first irrigation canal in the area. "This was just a desert then," he said. The area still looks like a desert, but there is a series of irrigation ditches between Hassan's house and the river, and the land around them is fertile and tilled. Hassan's grandfather held the title of *arbob*—headman—which he passed down to his son, Hassan's father. Hassan explained that the title is no longer used. He is called Commander, he says, because of the war and because he leads soldiers, but he retains a social rank equivalent to or greater than that of his forefathers. "There are no more *arbobs*," he said.

Hassan explained that his duty as a commander is to provide security, and that during the years of jihad against the Soviets he also had to act as a judge. "Normally, there are courts, laws, and judges," he said, "but during the war, if someone killed someone else, then it was my responsibility to deal with these people. A commander must be educated and understand about courts and laws. Before the fighting, I didn't understand anything about courts, laws, or human rights, but later, after I took charge of Dasht-i-Qala, I sought out advice, and now I understand." His teacher, he says, was a Muslim priest who was killed in fighting among the mujahideen. "In those days, I rode around on a horse and we had no courts or anything, but now we have courts and laws."

There is, apparently, a good deal of overlap between the duties of a commander and those of the son of the district's former *arbob*. Once a month, Hassan and the three other commanders of the Kokcha Union meet with delegates from the villages and towns in their communities to discuss problems, hear proposals, and seek agreement on actions to be taken. "We try to see how we can help the people," he said, "and most of them give their sons to us to be soldiers."

As a child, Hassan listened to his father's stories about fighting the Russians in the nineteen-twenties, when the Central Asian republics were forced into the new U.S.S.R. There was a Tajik revolt against the Russian Communists. "The Russians forced the Tajiks into Afghanistan, and my father joined in their guerrilla raids. I wanted to grow up to be a fighter like that. But now I am tired of fighting." He says that when he was young Dasht-i-Qala was a very different kind of place. "We had everything we needed, even though we lived in a small village. We had schools, peace. There were several companies doing business here. But then the Russians crossed the Amu Dar'ya, and the people of Dasht-i-Qala took their children and fled into the mountains, and many of them died. At the time, I had only ten men with guns, and when I reached where the people were at sunrise the next morning, I found women and children there, dead under the snow. It is one of my most terrible memories."

During the jihad against the Soviets, Hassan and his men hid out in a forested section of the mountains east of Dasht-i-Qala, in the neighboring district of Rostaq, from which they carried out raids. "There were only animals there, goats and things," he said. "It is a hard place to get to—twelve hours by horse from Dasht-i-Qala. We had a big underground cave, several guns, and five Russian jeeps. I spent fourteen years there. The Soviets tried to attack us several times in the summer, but they were unable to get close to us. One winter, though, in the snow, they came right up, wearing white, and we didn't see them. They laid siege to us for three months and tried to starve us out, but even then we knew ways to obtain food. And in the end they weren't able to get us."After the Soviets withdrew from Afghanistan in 1989, leaving the puppet government of President Najibullah in place, Hassan helped lead the mujahideen's successful military campaign to reconquer Taloqan. This was managed with the collusion of two Najib commanders who decided to switch sides. In their joint offensive, they killed the top government commander in Taloqan and seized the city. From then until 1992, when Najibullah's government fell to the mujahideen, Takhar Province was one of the main mujahideen bases in Afghanistan.

Hassan has four brothers. Two of them, he said, were killed by the Soviets, along with his mother and five of his nephews. He said that his mother was killed in reprisal for his mujahideen activities. He was in the mountains, and one night he sneaked down to her house and she slaughtered a lamb and fed him and his men. Hassan said that the Russians heard about this and came to her and asked if he had been there. She said no, but they killed her anyway. Within two months, his two brothers were also dead. "The person who helped the Russians"—that is, the man who informed them about Hassan's visit to his mother's house—"was a relative who lived nearby," Hassan said. "The mujahideen had killed his father, and this was his way of taking vengeance. Later, we caught him and I said to him, 'We killed your father and you killed my mother and that's the end of it.' We ended things there." When I expressed surprise at his merciful gesture, he laughed. "Now I am amazed at what I did. But, because of it, this place is secure and no one threatens me or wants to kill me."

Hassan told me that he had also employed conciliatory tactics in 1992, when Dasht-i-Qala reverted to his control. He called an assembly, a *jalsa,* which lasted two or three days. The area had been bitterly divided between non-Communists and pro-Communists. He proposed that they leave their rancor behind and rebuild their communities under a single commander—him. That is why, he repeated, "Dasht-i-Qala is a secure place and at peace and no one wants to kill me."

HASSAN'S WIVES WEAR BURKHAS, the extreme, head-to-toe coverings that the Taliban require and that are common in

Northern Alliance territory also. "We must follow our customs," Hassan says. But he doesn't necessarily favor them. "Why is it that in Mecca, the holiest Islamic place, women go with their faces uncovered—and men, too, wear nothing on their heads? If that is the center of Islam, then why don't they wear burkhas?" He concluded, with a rueful smile, "I think the burkha is just an old-fashioned Afghan custom."

One afternoon in Dasht-i-Qala, two women, one in a deep-violet burkha and the other wearing emerald green, floated past, briefly enlivening the backdrop of beat-up olive-green military vehicles, brown desert, and dusty shop fronts. The sight of women, or at least discernibly human creatures in feminine clothes, is about the only thing that relieves the harshness of the landscape. The visible part of Afghan society is unremittingly male, as is the land, which is drab and muscular. There is nothing soft about anything here, none of the creature comforts a Westerner takes for granted. Dust clogs your throat and coats hair and skin, and the people, who cover their faces with scarves and turbans, have learned to live with it in much the same way the British have grown used to rain. Much of northern Afghanistan today is a preindustrial society, without electricity, running water, or telephones. There are not even toys for the children. Water is pumped by hand from wells that have been dug with shovels, and roads are made by crews who break rocks and produce gravel with sledgehammers. Barefoot boys walk back and forth through beds of harvested rice, turning the grains with their toes to dry them in the sun. In the bazaars, porters carry poles with reed baskets on the ends, filled with everything from water to rock salt, which is sold in pinkish-gray chunks before being ground down to powder. Lambs are tethered next to men with long knives who slaughter them and hang the carcasses from hooks, hacking them into a steadily diminishing mess of blood and meat and bone and fat by day's end. Grain and vegetables are weighed in tin scales that are balanced with stones. On market days, people walk from distant villages—some even cross Taliban lines—to buy livestock (donkeys, camels, cattle, and horses) and then they herd the animals back home. The flat horizon is dotted with robed men riding donkeys, others on camel-back, and the odd motorbike spitting up clouds of dust.

There is a new primary school for boys and girls in the village of Nawabad, a couple of miles from Dasht-i-Qala. Six hundred boys study in the morning, and the girls, four hundred and thirty of them, come to class in the afternoon. They study the Koran and Islamic religion, history, mathematics, and geography. Some of the older children are learning English. Most of them come from families who fled the Taliban's military advance last year, when they seized Taloqan and the area right up to the Kokcha River. A couple of hundred displaced families still live in miserable little shacks on a scorching wasteland just outside the village, but some five thousand families have been resettled with host families by NGOs. The school is supported by Unicef, which pays the salaries of the teachers, and Shelter Now International, which built the latrines and provides some of the classroom materials. The school opened in May; many of the girls had not been in a classroom since they fled their hometowns and villages, where the Taliban had closed all their schools.

I visited the school a half hour or so before the day's classes ended. In twelve separate rooms off a mud court-yard, girls in headscarves sat on reed mats, reciting their lessons in unison. The teachers, mostly young women in

their late teens and early twenties, stood in front of black-
boards, their heads uncovered. Each of them held a twig
switch, as a pointer, and as I entered classrooms or passed
by doorways, many of them froze, or shifted their scarves.
I asked Headmaster Muhamadi if one of the teachers might
be willing to speak to me, and he said no, that was not a
good idea. Not because of them, or him, but because of
what people in the village would say.

The women teachers were beautiful, with large brown
eyes and fair skin. They wore colorful tunics, some of which
were decorated with flower patterns, and billowy pantaloons. One woman wore several gold bracelets, and most
of the women had dark kohl painted around their eyes.
When the classes ended and the students piled out from
the school through the mud doorway, the teachers slipped
silently down the dirt lane, garbed in white burkhas. They
had become wraiths, stumbling along on foot or riding
donkeys, bobbing away amid a throng of chattering, happy,
barefaced girls.

THE DAY OF THE FIRST AIR STRIKES, Mamur Hassan was in the
nearby town of Khoja Bahauddin, where the Northern Alliance defense ministry has its headquarters. He returned
around sunset and prayed with his lieutenants in the garden. Then everybody became somewhat frantic, and
Hassan rushed around between his house and the radio
room in the bungalow. When several men were getting
ready to leave in their jeeps and began making a lot of noise,
he shouted at them to be quiet and to remain on high alert
at their bases. He told one man that if he wasn't prepared
he would kill him. After they left, Hassan stood under the

plane tree, watching the sky above and looking at his wrist-watch, twitching with tension.

The men who stayed in the compound listened to Radio Tehran and the BBC's Farsi Service on shortwave radios. When reports of missile attacks began coming in, an exchange of tank and Katyusha rocket fire—baritone booms and clattery whooshes, respectively—could be heard in the distance. A dozen or so mujahideen stayed up most of the night, listening to the news and eavesdropping on enemy field-radio conversations. Hassan's personal secretary, Osman Muhammad, a twenty-four-year-old medical worker who had given up his job to fight the Taliban, had a long conversation on his radio with a Northern Alliance defector he knows. Osman explained to me that the man had had a misunderstanding with Qasi Qabir, Mamur Hassan's counterpart in Khoja Bahauddin, and had fled the district with his family. For the past two and half years, he had been serving as an officer with the Taliban near Taloqan. Osman said that he had called the man when the bombing began to say, "Come back now or else you will die." The defector had replied that it was too late, that there was no going back, that Qasi Qabir would kill him. Osman said that he had given him his personal guarantee of safety if he returned, but he admitted to me that the promise was worthless, and that Qasi Qabir would have the final say about the defector's fate. "It would be a big problem if Qasi Qabir found out the man came back and stayed here with Mamur Hassan," he said. "He would ask, 'Why are you protecting my enemy?' " I asked Osman if the defector agreed with the Taliban. "No, that's what's so terrible about this," he said. "He doesn't understand why fate has driven him into the arms of his enemies."

The next morning, I asked Mamur Hassan how he had slept. He chuckled and said he had watched TV and listened to the news until 1 A.M. He has a satellite dish and an aerial, and is thus one of only a few people in Dasht-i-Qala who can watch television. He said that if the Americans kept up their missile strikes and bombing raids the Taliban would go to the mountains to wage a guerrilla campaign. This was not his speculation, he said, but a plan already outlined by the Taliban. He also said that the Northern Alliance had an agreement with the Americans to launch a military offensive in tandem with their raids. Without the air strikes, Hassan said, the Northern Alliance would be able to do very little. He refused to be drawn out on the question of how anyone was going to defeat the Taliban in a guerrilla war in the mountains, although as a veteran of fourteen years in similar mountains he seemed qualified to comment.

"So," I said, "all this talk about finishing off the Taliban in a week once the bombing started was just hot air?" He smiled. "It was to boost the morale of the mujahideen. You understand. The fact of the matter is that the Taliban are very powerful. We need the air strikes in order to make any headway." He claimed that the Taliban had recently increased their troop strength along the hundred or so kilometres of the Takhar Province front line from fifteen thousand to twenty-five thousand soldiers. "This will give you some idea of what we face." Hassan said that if the Americans were able to inflict real damage with the air strikes and if they and the Russians would give the Northern Alliance the military equipment they had promised, then the Taliban could be taken down in a couple of months. "General Fahim has told me to collect all my soldiers and to be at the ready. But it is very difficult for me. I have food for only six hundred men and I have one thousand to feed. So the conditions are not right for a sustained attack. The truth is this. In these conditions, it's impossible."

HASSAN HAD PROMISED to introduce me to Sadruddin, the man who betrayed him and caused his mother's death during the years of the jihad. Sadruddin is forty-five, but he looks closer to sixty, a thin man with a goatee and a deeply furrowed, weather-beaten face. He arrived one morning a few days after the air strikes began. Sadruddin is Mamur Hassan's second cousin, and he is married to Hassan's niece. I asked him to tell me his version of the story. Had Mamur Hassan killed his father? Yes, Sadruddin said, although Hassan did not give the order. The leader of the mujahideen group that Hassan belonged to at the time had ordered him to capture Sadruddin's father, a well-off landowner, and six others like him from the Dasht-i-Qala area. They took them back to their cave in the mountains of Rostaq, where the mujahideen commander executed them with a pistol. He killed them, Sadruddin says, not because they were pro-Soviet but because they were influential and wealthy people, and he was jealous and afraid of their power. "My father was a good man, and many people followed him. When he died, I was just a boy, and all the responsibility of my family fell upon me." He said that his desire for vengeance was so great that he joined the army of the Najibullah regime. "After I joined the Najib government, I told my soldiers to kill Mamur Hassan's mother." Had he been present at the execution? "Yes," he acknowledged. "But I stood some distance away. We killed her with guns."

Mamur Hassan had been unable to retaliate immediately, Sadruddin said, but "when Najib fell, and Ahmed Shah Massoud occupied this valley, Mamur Hassan became the mujahideen commander, and I fled with thirty-five soldiers to a village that we secured. Mamur Hassan laid siege to us. I held out for four days, until an assembly of *arbobs*, led by Mamur Hassan's father, who was the most respected of all of them, arranged a reconciliation between us. We resolved our differences then, and have been friends ever since. Afterward, all of my soldiers joined the mujahideen, under the command of Mamur Hassan, and later I married his niece." Sadruddin didn't think that this was all that anomalous. "In the Holy Koran it says that if someone kills someone in your family, then you must kill that person. It also preaches forgiveness." Sadruddin is a wheat farmer now. "No more war for me," he said.

From: Jon Lee 10/15/2001

Hi. Am now with Thomas in Faizabad, which is like a muddy medieval camp, surrounded by junipers and mulberry trees. We arrived dusty but well. Are in Guesthouse Number One, beside a rushing river that furrows beneath great yellow mountains. Ramadan is approaching, and at night the air is brittle and chill, but the days are sunny, with cloudless blue skies. On the way here, just before crossing over a canyon via a narrow bridge made of old Russian tank treads—the frontier between Takhar Province and Badakhshan—we came on three mujahideen testing the guns of a T-55 tank. The man sitting at the machine gun asked where I was from. When I said that I was an American, he began leering at me and swivelled the gun in my direction. "And I am from Afghanistan," he said. "Look what we did to New York!" I told our translator to tell him something along the lines of: "If you had been part of the attack on New York you would not be here because you would be dead." The Afghan's response was, "Tell the American that if he wants to kill me, fine. But I will kill him too." His companions began urging him to lay off, but he blustered for a while longer. "What have the American air strikes accomplished?" he asked. And I said, "And what have you mujahideen accomplished all these years? Here you are, play-

38

ing with your tank, and the Taliban are in power in Kabul." The translator said he didn't want to interpret any longer, and Thomas interceded. This was just the latest of several such exchanges I've had
with Afghans recently. Their resentment about the bombing campaign, plus the lack of new aid coming to the Northern Alliance, is
seeping to the surface.

Last night, when we were in Rostaq, at the Shelter Now compound, I was told that the local mullah had said to his flock that the
American bombing was killing civilians and was a bad thing. There
were rumors in town that American planes had hit a school in
Taloqan two days ago. Before we left Dasht-i-Qala, one of the warlords I had been interviewing—the imperious one with the sunglasses—had made the point explicitly. "We understand that the
Americans are bombing Afghanistan because they are fighting terrorism," he said. "And we are against terrorism too. But if the Americans were not here fighting against terrorism, we would be fighting
against them."

From: Jon Lee 10/16/2001
I met a man, Walid, who is well-connected in the Afghan government here. He has a friend in Mazar-i-Sharif with a radio, and the
friend tells him that Mazar could fall any day. The top Taliban commanders have already fled. Walid says that when Mazar falls, the
Taliban who control the border with Uzbekistan will retreat to
Kunduz and make a stand there. This is consistent with what Mamur
Hassan was telling me. In any case, I think Thomas and I should be
prepared to get to Mazar when the time comes, which means we
will have to go through Uzbekistan. I'll need new letters for an Uzbek
visa. Copies should also be sent to Liza Faktor in Moscow, who
thinks she can move things from there. In the story of the fall of a
city like Mazar, the goatfuck media competition is less of a hindrance
than it is here. There will, in other words, be plenty for everyone.
But timing is of the essence.

Tomorrow I'll try to find a good spot outside of town for phone signals. If I'm successful, I'll try calling you early Thursday my time.

From: Jon Lee 10/21/2001
The plane expected today from Dushanbe, as with every day since last Tuesday, did not arrive (too hazy, supposedly). But maybe tomorrow. People are coming and going overland in both directions, which takes two days, including hassles and delays from the Russian border guards. If the plane does not fly in and out tomorrow or Tuesday latest, I think the only option is to stay here and close the piece. Traveling by road to Dushanbe would waste too much time.

Julius Strauss of the Daily Telegraph has an Inmarsat phone, which is big and clumsy and expensive, but the system has clear signals pretty much everywhere (as compared to the more portable and less expensive Iridium). He says we can use it this week. You can call me on it in the evenings, my time, which costs him nothing. If necessary I can call you, although that does cost something. In other words, we should have a fail-safe communications link for editing the new piece if I am unable to get out of here. The other good thing about his phone is that it can be used indoors. I don't have to go outside to get a signal.

The journalists in Uzbekistan, by the way, seem to be cooped up and not allowed anywhere near the border. Of course this may change when and if Mazar-i-Sharif falls. But there doesn't seem to be a new story for us there just now. I'll pick up the Uzbek visa in Dushanbe, just to have it. So that if we decide that I should return to Europe to get a new sat phone, I could come back at the drop of a hat if necessary.

If I leave, Thomas will probably stick around in northern Afghanistan, and we can keep in touch.

From: Jon Lee 10/23/2001
No plane again today. Julius Strauss is going to Dasht-i-Qala, and since he has our backup communications and the means to send Thomas's photos, I think we should stick close to him. I will set out after my interview with President Rabbani's son, so I won't arrive in Dasht-i-Qala until early evening. I will try to call you at our usual time, en route. Will stick around through the closing of the piece, and, if it seems the thing to do, will move overland toward Dushanbe on Friday or Saturday. We can discuss.

From: Jon Lee 10/24/2001
It rained all night, and more of the mountains just above have snow. I heard that the Panjshir is snowed in, and that the journos left there have to be choppered out. There are supposedly 170 of them on a waiting list.

From: Jon Lee 10/25/2001
I am in the hotel in Dushanbe, at a small bank of computer terminals in the foyer, downloading the proof. Will call you when I have read it. Long story about how I got here. The plane that arrived unexpectedly this morning turned out to be going to the Tajik military airport and it was hell to get out of there to Dushanbe proper.

From: Jon Lee 10/25/2001
Please send file as a pasted e-mail message. The attachments you are sending come out in Cyrillic. I cannot make data connection using the sat phone, which is upstairs. I can only use it outside, on the balcony. Sorry.

From: Jon Lee 10/25/2001
OK. I have it now. Have downloaded it onto a floppy and will go to my room to read it, where I have phone in hand to talk to you. Will call in half an hour. Sorry for the hassles.

In the Court of the Pretender

One afternoon in the crowded bazaar in Faizabad, a muddy town of about a hundred thousand people in the far northeastern corner of Afghanistan, I came upon a stall where weapons were being sold. A good submachine gun was available for the equivalent of four hundred and eighty dollars, and there was a derringer in a shoulder holster, and ammunition. I was trying to have a conversation with the arms merchant when a worn-looking man appeared at my side and began to help translate. He spoke, with some effort, a curiously literary English with an Irish-sounding accent, and as we walked among the stalls of the bazaar he explained that he had been a journalist in Kabul until the Taliban closed down all the media. "Now I am jobless," he said, "and a displaced person." I was attracting quite a lot of attention by that time, as *kafirs,* or unbelievers —white-skinned non-Afghans—usually do. Dozens of children and men were crowding around, gaping and chattering. A soldier in a green jacket, camouflage pants, and black boots walked alongside us, wielding a short leather crop with which he whacked people who came too close to me. "The mujahideen are no different from the Taliban," my new companion said under his breath. He was referring to the soldier when he said "mujahideen," which is the general term for the Muslim fighters who participated in the jihad against the Soviets in the nineteen-eighties, and who are now fighting the Taliban. This particular mujahideen wore the uniform of the Islamic State of Afghanistan, the government that fled Kabul when the Taliban took over, in 1996. The members of the government-in-exile are now part of the Northern Alliance, the main anti-Taliban opposition. "The government is fundamentalist," the former journalist muttered. "The only difference is who is in power and who isn't. The problem is Islam, you know. It's like a drug." He told me that he would meet me the next day, that he had things he wanted to say, and he slipped into the crowd.

Faizabad is the capital of Badakhshan Province, which shares a mountainous border with Tajikistan on the north and Pakistan on the east. A panhandle of the province extends northeast for nearly two hundred miles, past the part of Kashmir controlled by Pakistan, and then on to the border with China. The Soviets seized Faizabad when they invaded Afghanistan in December 1979. They simply rolled their tanks across the Tajikistan border and established a base at the airstrip outside of town. Perhaps six thousand troops were stationed there. The mujahideen took control after the Soviets left, ten years later, and I was told that they went on a looting and burning rampage. The ruins of several government complexes are still visible.

Traders' caravans have passed through Faizabad for centuries. Smugglers still hawk their wares in the bazaar, a serpentine track lined with stalls of cloth merchants, shoemakers, and tailors working at old-fashioned hand-operated Butterfly sewing machines. The pelts of wolves, foxes, mink, lynx, and even snow leopards hang next to hand-wrought adzes, pickaxes, hatchets, and oxen plows. Money changers in the bazaar know with precision the current rates for American dollars, afghanis, and Iranian and Saudi rials. I met an eighteen-year-old boy there one day who had just arrived in town after walking over the mountains from Pakistan for a week. He was on the way, he said, to Germany, where an older brother lives. The boy was being helped by a network of relatives who had underworld contacts in Central Asia and Russia. Such people pass through Faizabad all the time, using the same routes by which arms and ammunition come into Afghanistan and by which opium and heroin flow out of it.

Burhanuddin Rabbani, the president of the Islamic State of Afghanistan—which still controls the country's seat in the UN, even though it hasn't controlled much else for some time—was born in Faizabad, and when the Taliban drove him out of Kabul he and his mujahideen fighters fled north, to Mazar-i-Sharif and Taloqan, and finally to his hometown. Faizabad seems like a medieval city, and Rabbani's place in it is similar to that of a theocratic vizier or khan. The streets—dirt lanes, actually—are full of refugees, pale children with running sores, beggars in rags, elderly Tajik and Uzbek men clad in long winter tunics, mujahideen with guns, and women concealed by burkhas. Cows, donkeys, and the occasional horse wander about. Many of the tradesmen have hooped wooden cages that contain partridges. They keep them for *kawk tangi* fights, an ancient sport that is played in the spring.

There is almost no modern urban infrastructure in Faizabad. Most vehicles belong to the government and the mujahideen or to foreign aid organizations, although there are a few traders' trucks with colorful wooden bulwarks. A tiny, Russian-built television station serves some five thousand TV sets, and a beat-up and out-of-date electrical generator produces a few hours of weak electricity every four days. An ancient windup-telephone system operates through a switchboard. Several men, working in a large shed, hand-set a biweekly government newspaper—one folded sheet printed in Farsi, with a circulation of five hundred. The printing machines, which are from India, East Germany, and Romania, are museum pieces from the age of steel and iron foundries. Water is produced by rudimentary waterwheels or hand-pumped from open wells and carried by men and boys with buckets hanging from poles resting on their shoulders. Rubbish is dumped pretty much everywhere, and, while some people have outhouse latrines, a great many people—men, at least—defecate out of doors. The stench in certain quarters of the city, particularly around ruined houses, vacant lots, and along stretches of the riverbank, is overwhelming.

PRESIDENT RABBANI'S HOME IS, by Faizabad standards, luxurious. It is a two-story, tin-roofed house set behind a high stone-and-concrete wall on a back alleyway up the hill from the bazaar, in the Old City. The house is painted a pale blue, and there are iron railings on the verandas. Mujahideen sentinels are stationed outside. When Rabbani leaves the house, he travels in a convoy of two black Toyota Land Cruisers surrounded by gunmen. I interviewed him one afternoon in a bungalow called the Star Hotel, a few minutes from his house, where senior Northern Alliance officials work and live and which also serves as a kind of reception house for Rabbani. It was built on stone ramparts overlooking the Kokcha River, and you get to it on foot over a narrow concrete causeway. In the late afternoon, men fish from the causeway, and boys play games of volleyball on a nearby sandbar. Two soldiers carefully frisk visitors to the building and then inspect all their belongings. Items such as cigarette lighters, knives, and battery-operated flashlights are politely confiscated. Extra security precautions have been taken since September 9, when Massoud was assassinated. The assassins had interviewed Rabbani in the Panjshir Valley a few days before they traveled to Massoud's headquarters in Khoja Bahauddin.

A room in the Star Hotel has been set up for Rabbani's appearances. The floor is covered with a red carpet and the ceiling is draped with a cheap flowery fabric. Velvety armchairs are lined up against the walls, and at one end of the room, next to a flag stand with the banner of the Islamic State of Afghanistan, a chair has been placed for the president. Just in front, a low table is decorated with little vases filled with plastic flowers. The windows look out to the roiling, boulder-filled waters of the Kokcha, and the sound of rushing water penetrates the room.

The interview was scheduled for three o'clock, but Rabbani was an hour and a half late, and two of his senior minions—smooth young English-speaking men who wore Western clothes and had what looked like blow-dried hairdos—kept me company. Another aide began glancing pointedly at his watch after we had been standing in the room for more than an hour. "He must be busy with the Queen," the man said sarcastically. I was a little surprised, and asked him what people in Faizabad thought of Rabbani. "Except for a few commanders and these people"—he nodded his head toward the two minions with the hairdos— "he is hated by everyone." The man kept his voice low and watched to make sure that the loyalists were out of ear-

Burhanuddin Rabbani leads a group of mujahideen in prayer at sunset in Faizabad.

shot. "People are fed up with him," he said. He explained that there had been no love lost between Rabbani and Massoud, and that there was a power struggle going on between Massoud's followers and Rabbani's. Massoud's official successor, General Fahim, had not yet managed to assume full command, and the situation was particularly tense because of the machinations involving the United States and the attempt to construct a "post-Taliban" government. Even some of Rabbani's relatives didn't want him to be president again. "Things have changed dramatically," the aide said, since Massoud's death, "and no one knows what will happen tomorrow." He then moved discreetly away to stand on the opposite side of the room.

A few moments later, Rabbani entered the hallway leading to the room, his two aides scurrying along in half crouches in front of him, holding their hands on their hearts. Rabbani is in his early sixties. He has pale skin, and his beard is white and immaculately trimmed. He was wearing a pair of smart black leather loafers, a beige *shalwar kameez*—the tunic and loose pants that most Afghan men wear—and a camel-colored woollen waistcoat under a black-and-white herringbone blazer. His turban was white with black stripes. As he came into the room, he greeted me with a brief, friendly nod and said, in English, "Good afternoon." Then he sat in his armchair and awaited my questions. His responses consisted mostly of a litany of Taliban perfidies and a long soliloquy about his past good intentions, which had been sadly frustrated by the Taliban's seizure of power.

Rabbani said that the Taliban's radical and violent interpretation of Islam under the guise of Sharia law was in fact nothing but an extremist application of a tribal code. I asked him to explain for me the brand of Islam that he had tried to establish when he was president—from 1992, when the mujahideen ousted the Afghan government that the Soviets had installed, until 1996, when the Taliban came in. He was vague on details, and said, a little defensively, "As you know, while I was president, because of the constant infighting I was unable to enforce Islamic law in a way that could benefit and advance Afghan society." Rabbani talked about the things he had tried to do: he had signed an amnesty for his former Communist foes; allowed political parties and a diverse media to operate freely; he had promoted foreign investment; rebuilt the war-damaged University of Kabul; encouraged female participation in teaching and banking jobs. Many other projects were still in the planning stages. "Unhappily, the ongoing civil war has not allowed us to take the practical steps to implement these projects," he said.

I asked Rabbani why, in the part of Afghanistan under his control, women wore the burkha. "The burkha is not a part of the Islamic tradition," he said. "When I was on the religious law faculty"—at the University of Kabul in the late sixties and early seventies—"I designed a new form of dress appropriate for female students that covered the head and shoulders, but left the face and hands exposed. Unfortunately, because of the coup, we were unable to take the matter further. Here the burkha is worn because of tradition. Because of the insecurity of the war situation, women are afraid not to wear it, but afterward they will be free not to use the burkha if they wish."

After about forty-five minutes of this sort of thing, Rabbani took his leave. The next day, I met with the man who had spoken about a rift between Massoud and Rabbani. "Massoud's people now suspect Rabbani and Abdul Rasul Sayyaf"—a mujahideen commander stationed in the Panjshir Valley—"of being behind the assassination," he said.

Sayyaf has a bad reputation because in the nineteen-eighties he was closely allied with Arabs, particularly the Saudis. He gave the Arab assassins safe passage through Northern Alliance territory and helped them get an audience with Massoud, during which they set off a bomb hidden around one man's waist. Faizabad is full of conspiracy theories and skeptical glosses on events, and my informant, who told me that his name is Walid (a pseudonym, as are several other names here), was not the only person who gave me a version of the story of Rabbani's alleged complicity in Massoud's murder. Rabbani, on the other hand, told me that the assassins had wanted to kill him and Sayyaf as well as Massoud, and had tried to get all three of them together for a photograph.

IDRIS, THE FORMER JOURNALIST who said that Islam is like a drug, came to the government guest house where I was staying the day after we met in the bazaar. He suggested that we walk down by the river, and when we were out of earshot of the official minders he said that we could sit next to the ruined concrete bridge, and that if anyone asked what we were discussing we would say it was the history of the bridge. So we sat on a pile of broken masonry and Idris talked about his despair. He didn't care if he got into trouble for speaking to me. "I am tired of this life," he said, "and I am willing to be sacrificed. I am against fundamentalism of all kinds. I am against Islam, and when the Soviets were in Afghanistan I was also against Communism, which I think is a kind of fundamentalism." I asked him about President Rabbani. "Rabbani is a fundamentalist just like the Taliban," he said, and then he began to whisper. "Rabbani is secretly trying to make a deal with the Taliban, except for the Arabs who are in Afghanistan." He meant excluding Osama bin Laden's people. I asked Idris how he knew this, and he said that someone who worked closely with Rabbani had told him that overtures had taken place. Idris explained that Rabbani hoped to return to power as the head of a "moderate" fundamentalist regime made up of his allies and "acceptable" Taliban figures.

This, again, was a version of a story I'd heard from others, some of whom have more authoritative credentials than Idris does. In the public discussions about creating a coalition of factions that would form a government if or when the Taliban are crushed, Rabbani has guardedly supported the involvement of King Zahir Shah, whom the Americans and the Pakistanis are encouraging to convene a Loya Jirga, a grand national council that would choose a leader. But Walid said it is well known that Rabbani would never be elected by the Loya Jirga, and that he is secretly forming alliances to counter the king's coalition. The king is an ethnic Pashtun—that is, a member of a group from which, historically, Afghanistan's rulers have been drawn. The Taliban and most people who live in the southern part of Afghanistan are also Pashtuns. The mujahideen who formed a government in Kabul in 1992 and now make up the Northern Alliance are mostly ethnic Tajiks, like Rabbani and Uzbeks.

A few days after our interview, President Rabbani went to Dushanbe, the capital of Tajikistan, to meet with the Russian president, Vladimir Putin, who was on his way home from Shanghai, where he had met with President Bush. Walid told me later that Putin had assured Rabbani that he was the most acceptable candidate for the presidency and had encouraged him not to support the king. "Of course, Rabbani does not need convincing about this," Walid said. According to Walid, Putin has been playing a double game with the Americans, as has Rabbani. But the meeting in Dushanbe clarified Putin's opposition to Taliban participation in a coalition government, and presumably Rabbani's gestures to the Taliban have ceased. Russia stepped up its military support for the Northern Alliance, and the first major shipment of new war matériel had just been handed over. "Russia provided the United Front"— the official name of the Northern Alliance—"with forty-five million dollars' worth of different weapons. Eight tanks, a remarkable amount of ammunition, and heavy and light weapons crossed the Tajik border into Afghanistan," Walid said. No helicopters were included in this package, he said, although Rabbani has been promised a further seventy-five million dollars' worth of hardware, including more tanks, helicopters, and new antiaircraft guns. The present understanding with Russia seems to be that Rabbani would lead a post-Taliban government that would include Afghan technocrats now living abroad—these presumably picked by the Americans, and perhaps including some of Zahir Shah's people. "Rabbani is very pleased," Walid said.

DURING OUR CHAT by the river, Idris explained why he distrusted Rabbani. "When Rabbani was president," he said, "we had to wear beards, to pray all the time. Now he is weak, and so he is trying to put on a good face to the world, but if he becomes strong again he will do the same. He is a fundamentalist!" Idris is thirty-eight, although, like most

Afghan men, he looks much older. He grew up in a rural district not far from Faizabad and studied journalism in Kabul in the nineteen-eighties. After he graduated, he served for three years in the military, during the government of Muhammad Najibullah, the Afghan Communist whom the Soviets made president in the late eighties, and who remained in power until he was ousted by the mujahideen in 1992. Idris wrote for army publications, and afterward worked for a newspaper that he describes as impartial. When Kabul fell to the mujahideen, however, he fled to Pakistan, fearing that he might be killed. He returned to Afghanistan two years ago. He has four children, ranging in age from three to thirteen. "How did you manage to have all those children if you were out of the country?" I asked him. He laughed, and explained that he had returned to Afghanistan several times, clandestinely, by walking over the border at Chitral—a timeworn smugglers' route—and sneaking back home. He would enter his village at night, he said, and not leave the house until it was time to go back to Pakistan. He came home to stay because after his last visit his wife had been beaten and interrogated by the local mujahideen commander. His family still lives in the village, and since he cannot get work he is finding it hard to spend time with them. He says they nearly died of hunger eight months ago. He came to Faizabad to see if he could find work as a translator for a Western journalist.

When I suggested to Idris that it must have been very hard for his wife all those years that he was away, he assured me that he had her total support, and that, like him, she is educated, and is in agreement with his views. He said that they have been teaching their children not to believe in Islam, although they understand that they must pay lip service to religion in school. He said that he had thought about naming his son Salman, after Salman Rushdie, "but some of my friends convinced me that this was not a good idea."

While he was in Pakistan, Idris survived by translating books from Urdu, which he learned while he was there, along with English. I ended up spending several days in Faizabad with him, and he always carried a Farsi-English dictionary and would ask me to explain the difference between similar terms—between "fornication" and "adultery," for instance. Idris said that Islam is like "a cave"—he pulled out the Farsi-English dictionary to find the word he wanted—which is "full of bacteria." I remarked that life must be extremely hard for him, being alone in a land such as this. "Well, you know, there are a lot of people in Afghanistan who hate Islam, but they cannot show their faces," he said. He described himself as a humanist, and said he had read a lot: "Goethe, Jean-Paul Sartre, Victor Hugo, Jean-Jacques Rousseau, and Albert Camus." Also American writers like Faulkner and Steinbeck, he added. "It helped me open my eyes and look at the sky of the world." He had written a book about Islam, unpublished, of course. It was critical of the Koran, and of the Prophet Muhammad, whom he described as an illiterate shepherd. The book was titled, he said, translating roughly from the Farsi, "The Crazy Dogs of Certain Centuries."

Idris is an iconoclast, and, for Afghanistan, an extraordinary man—brave to the point of foolhardiness. In this context, in fact, he could be regarded as half mad, and perhaps he is. He is well read, and an atheist, he understands that life can be different, and he is desperately clinging to his beliefs in a poverty-stricken charnel house that is ruled by illiterate gunmen, brutish warlords, and superstitious mullahs.

*   *   *

THERE IS A LARGE GRAFFITO on a wall along the main road into Faizabad that says, in English, "Production Sale and Use of Opium Is Strongly Forbidden by Islam." A similar declamation is painted on a ruined building at the airport. One can't help getting the impression that these are Potemkin-style diktats designed to please workers for United Nations agencies and Western aid organizations who go in and out of town. Opium is the most important crop in Afghanistan, not least for the mujahideen, who got into the business in the eighties, during the jihad against the Soviets. Last year, according to the CIA, Afghanistan produced seventy percent of the world's opium. Much of it is said to go through Faizabad. After I had been in town for a few days, I met a man who works for one of the foreign aid organizations and who explained to me how some of the trafficking works. "A lot of opium is grown in Badakhshan Province," he said. "And some is purchased from local people on both sides of the front lines"—where the Taliban and the Northern Alliance are fighting. "It's mostly sent out in raw form and then refined in Tajikistan and sent to the West through Moscow." He said that last year, when he was helping distribute wheat to refugees near the front line on the Kokcha River, near the border with Tajikistan, he had seen donkeys ferrying opium between the Taliban and Northern Alliance sides. The Northern Alliance commanders and the Taliban arranged the exchanges by radio, he said. "Some of them had friendly contacts, even though they were fighting one another." Helicopters from Tajikistan picked up the opium at drop-off points near the border formed by the Amu Dar'ya River. The aid worker said that last year there was an official ban on opium trafficking, but that "no real practical steps have been taken." He smiled. The ban was a "nine-day wonder," good for public relations.

I also discussed the opium situation with Muhammad Nazir Shafiee, President Rabbani's foreign-relations adviser and a member of the President's Commission for the Fight Against Drugs and Narcotics. Nazir is twenty-seven years old. He was one of the aides who had held his hand over his heart as he escorted Rabbani into the room at the Star Hotel for our interview. He explained that Rabbani's government had been confiscating drugs, arresting traffickers, and destroying opium fields. But, he added, the Islamic State of Afghanistan also had to deal with drought, war, and the influx of displaced people from both plagues. The UN and other international aid organizations had not helped them much with crop-substitution programs for the affected farmers. Nazir blamed the opium trafficking and the heroin trade on ethnic Pashtuns, and on the Taliban. He was especially critical of Pakistan. "In Faizabad, there has only been one crime in the past twelve months—a theft from one shop. The people here are not familiar with international criminal activity—this comes from Pakistan. The Pakistanis, you know, will sell their own mothers for four thousand rupees."

Nazir also complained that whenever UN officials or foreign diplomats came to northern Afghanistan they were critical because women wore burkhas. "They don't have to wear burkhas," he said. "Women are free to do what they want here." He attributed the burkha-wearing phenomenon to social pressures. He denied claims that Rabbani first imposed the burkha when he became president. "At the beginning of the Islamic State of Afghanistan, we were weak and had to make compromises and accept the participation of Gulbuddin Hekmatyar, a fundamentalist. He had Pakistan behind him, and he was raining rockets on Kabul. He made women wear burkhas, but it was not the policy of the Islamic State of Afghanistan. The West thinks we are fundamentalists, and that because we started the Islamic revolution we are dangerous. But we are reasonable Muslims, I tell you!" Nazir does not support the return of King Zahir Shah. "How can we accept this man who has spent the last twenty-eight years living a comfortable life in Rome? Did he come once to see the refugees in Pakistan during all the years of the jihad, even just to say hello? No, not once. Not for one day, not even one hour. He never came. And, before that, for forty years he was king of this country. He spent his time having a very good life, hunting, drinking, and playing with women. Did he make a road? Did he leave a factory that could make one of these?"—Nazir held up a ballpoint pen. "No! He left nothing." If there was any man qualified to run Afghanistan after the Taliban were thrown out, he said, it was Rabbani. And he hoped to go to Kabul and have a post—*inshallah,* God willing—in the future government with him.

Nazir explained that he owed his position and his rising influence in part to his late father, a religious scholar who had been chief justice for Rabbani's Jamiat-i-Islami Party and an old friend. His father was also Rabbani's law adviser during his presidency. Nazir is from an Afghan family of, as he put it, high standing. "We own twenty-four thousand acres of land," he said. "I have stamped documents from all the kings of Afghanistan over four centuries which says we are the owners." Under the Soviet-backed Communist regime, he said, the family's land was confiscated and split into many six-acre plots that were given to farmers. "We have recouped most of it." Four thousand people lived on the land as sharecroppers. The people in his district still treat him with deference and address him by the hereditary feudal title "Khan," but he doesn't like it. "I tell them not to, because I am a modern man, and I want to make my way with my own shoulders." If democracy returned to Afghanistan, he said, he hoped to go into politics himself, maybe by running for parliament. He would have a chance of winning, because of his family's influence. "We are not only economically powerful, you see; we have also been a very religious family, for centuries." So how high was he aiming? "First, parliament, and then who knows? I will see how far I can go."

ZARMEENA, AN AFGHAN WOMAN of about thirty, works for a foreign aid organization that has an office in the so-called New City, a spacious, dusty suburb of Faizabad where most of the NGOs have their compounds—although there are virtually no foreign workers left there. They fled the country after Massoud was killed and the World Trade Center was attacked. Zarmeena wears a burkha when she is in public, but inside her office she simply puts a scarf over her hair. She lived in Kabul through the years of Communist government and was there in 1992, when Najibullah fell and the mujahideen seized power. "The changes from Najib to Rabbani weren't so great," Zarmeena said, "except that the fighting went on, and every part of Kabul was controlled by a different mujahideen faction, and it was very difficult to move from one part of the city to the other. I lived in the area controlled by Rabbani and Massoud's men. When the Taliban came, I used to wear a big shawl with only my eyes showing. Then I heard that some women were being beaten in the city center for wearing the same kind of shawl, and so I put on the burkha. It is difficult to wear, especially for more than two or three hours; it is very hot inside, it is hard to walk, and you get a headache, because the top of it is so tight on your head."

Zarmeena was a medical student until that became no longer possible for women. "So then I got married," she said, with a laugh, "because I had nothing else to do, and a year after the Taliban took power we came here. When we arrived, it was more or less the same as Kabul. Women could be doctors and teachers, for instance, although they were not allowed to work with the Western NGOs. It was not looked well upon—that a woman would be working in an office together with men." Zarmeena was one of the first women to overcome that ban. As for the burkha, she believes that it is officially required in Northern Alliance territory. "I think it is a law." I told her that President Rabbani had said that Afghan women were free to go without it if they chose. Zarmeena smiled and raised her eyebrows. "I'd like to see him say that to a group of Afghan women," she said. Zarmeena was teaching English to some girls, and she had not yet got into trouble for that, although she knew people who had. "The way it works here, if I am very active —if I do things they don't like, like speaking out or participating in certain meetings—the mullahs will make remarks about me in the Friday prayers. The government supports the mullahs in this. It is a form of social control. And this is why women here do not take off the burkha." I asked her if she would go out without one. "It takes great courage to be the first," she said. "It would be very hard."

SALAHUDDIN RABBANI, the president's eldest son, is married to a woman who does not wear a burkha, although he said he hoped that I would not mention this. Salahuddin's wife and two children live in London, as did he until September 15, when he returned to Afghanistan to be with his father. Salahuddin is thirty years old and is the third of the president's ten children. He is a full-faced young man of medium build and height, darker-skinned than his father, with a faint goatee and dark hair parted in the middle. He wears frameless glasses, and has a modest-seeming, intelligent demeanor.

Salahuddin studied at the King Fahd University of Petroleum and Minerals in Dhahran from 1989 to 1995, and received a degree in marketing. He went to Pakistan, married an Afghan girl from a Pashtun family living in exile there, and moved to Dubai, where he started an import-export business, which he didn't particularly enjoy. He and his family then moved to London. He earned a degree in business management and was going to continue his studies, but now he thinks he should stay in Afghanistan. "I see my future here, as an Afghan trying to do something for his country," he said to me, adding, with a chuckle, "Now I just have to convince my wife."

Salahuddin came back, he said, because "the death of Massoud placed a huge burden on my father." He confirmed that Massoud had died when the bombs went off, but that his death was kept secret for almost a week because of the demoralizing effect it would have on the Northern Alliance fighters. The Taliban immediately launched an offensive. "They intended to take northern Afghanistan," he said, "and then Samarkand and Bukhara" —in Uzbekistan—and also advance into Tajikistan. "And, you know, they might have succeeded, because the Central Asian states are very weak. If the Russian border guards weren't stationed there, they might have fallen already."

Salahuddin describes his father as a moderate political figure. He recalled that in the nineteen-eighties, during the jihad against the Soviets in Afghanistan, his father went to Washington at the invitation of President Reagan: "He went at the height of anti-American feeling in the Muslim world, and was opposed by many Arab states who had been backing the mujahideen, and he even laid a wreath at the Tomb of the Unknown Soldier." Afterward, Salahuddin said, "These wealthy Arabs stopped supporting us, and they began calling my father 'the American.'"

I said to Salahuddin that it seemed clear to me that his father, for all his careful language on the matter, was against the return of King Zahir Shah, and he agreed. "This government is the legitimate government and is made up of people who fought for the country for many years. If Zahir Shah comes back, which forces will pave the way for him and protect him—the UN?" He objected to the criticism of the Northern Alliance as a group of ethnic minorities. "There is no majority people in Afghanistan," he said. The notion that Afghanistan had to be led by an ethnic Pashtun was a Pakistani concoction.

Salahuddin made much of what he perceived as the dilemma the Pakistanis were now in because of their interference in Afghanistan's affairs. "With the Taliban and Osama bin Laden, the Pakistanis put all of their eggs in one basket. Now they are looking for another force to represent their interests. In a sense, before the missile strikes, by being the one country trying to legitimatize the Taliban in the eyes of the international community, they were trying to get a UN seat for bin Laden." Salahuddin laughed.

"That would have been a real first. The first UN representation for an international terrorist."

Salahuddin, like Nazir, said that his father had not
been responsible for the introduction of the burkha and
other Islamic social restrictions. "My wife is a dental hy-
gienist," he said, "and currently a domestic engineer"—
this was said lightheartedly, meaning she was raising their
kids—"but if she wants to go to work I don't mind. My father did not impose the burkha. The burkha is an Afghan
custom. No one is telling women they must wear it." He
wouldn't let himself get drawn into a discussion of whether
or not it would be appropriate for his wife to test this view
of the situation if she came to Afghanistan, but when we
said good-bye, amid the attendants and bodyguards,
Salahuddin turned to me and said, "I hope when we next
meet it will be in Kabul"—he smiled—"and that there you
will see many women who are dressed only in scarves and
loose clothing, not in burkhas."

I MET A MAN in Faizabad, Dr. Rostum, who is what he described as a member of Afghanistan's educated urban intelligentsia. He is more than a decade older than Salahuddin,
and his experiences during the years that the Rabbani
government was in power—years that Salahuddin was out
of the country—did not conform with Salahuddin's recollections. Dr. Rostum came to Faizabad last year, when his
hometown fell to the Taliban. It was the fifth time in the
last six years that he had moved his family because of the
advancing war. He came to see me at the guest house one
afternoon just before sunset, and we went to the far end of
the garden to talk. We sat at one of the stone tables overlooking the Kokcha, under a big walnut tree.

Dr. Rostum was a medical student in Kabul and had graduated during the Communist regime in the mid-eighties. He has a beard and wears a *shalwar kameez,* but he said that he used to be clean-shaven and wear Western clothes. Then, in the early nineties, when Rabbani took power, men were required to have beards and pray five times a day and women were separated from men on public buses. "I am a Muslim," he said, "and sometimes I even go to the mosque to pray—but why should I be forced to go five times a day?" The transformation of Afghanistan began when the mujahideen were in Kabul, he said. He described a mujahideen commander ordering the destruction of the electrical generator in the town where he lived in northern Afghanistan. It was an act of vengeance against the Communists. "The commander said, 'The Communists say that history can never be turned back. But I will turn it back.' And he destroyed the generator." Dr. Rostum clasped his hands together tightly when he told me this story, recalling what it meant for his country.

"In the seventies," Dr. Rostum said, "life for me was going to school and being well dressed and thinking about the future. A doctor was a well-regarded person then, with a secure job in a hospital. Every morning, he shaved, and would dress in pants and a shirt and then he would drive to work in his own vehicle, or go by government transport. There was a government, and the government paid him a salary. He didn't have to work in other jobs, like being a baker, a salesman, or a clerk. He only had to be a doctor. But now in Faizabad there are doctors and science teachers who are making bricks, working as clerks, selling food in the bazaar. I personally hoped that when the mujahideen came to power, since they had been backed by foreign countries, they would bring modernity with them. But it was exactly the opposite of what I hoped." And then, when the Taliban came, things got even worse.

"When we were younger, under Zahir Shah"—in the sixties—"and later under Daoud"—who overthrew the king in 1973—"there were cinemas and theatres in Kabul and Kandahar, Herat and Mazar-i-Sharif and Jalalabad, and for ladies there was no pressure to wear burkhas. In those days, maybe one to two percent of the girls wore burkhas— they were from very conservative religious families. And they were not like the burkhas of today, which have come from Iran or Pakistan; they were more like long veils. My father was a small trader who made trips to Kabul. My brothers and I begged him to bring us a radio, and, when he did, our house was like a wedding party for three months. All of our neighbors would come over to hear the news and listen to music." Dr. Rostum smiled as he recalled that the radio had played every morning from six to eight, then at lunchtime from twelve to one, and in the evenings from six to nine. "When Daoud came to power in Afghanistan, the education was great, it was the golden time for education. And at the end of his time he brought us a TV station. It was a very new thing for us, to see people announcing the news, watching films, and singing songs. And even after the Soviet invasion, in the cities that were controlled by the government, things continued mostly as usual. The educational system continued and received the support of the government. There were lots of books, as well, even if these came mostly from the Soviet bloc. The way things are today, it is as if Afghanistan had stepped back a hundred years in time."

I asked Dr. Rostum if he was depressed. "Yes," he said. "Very depressed. I want to live, to have a comfortable life. What is that? To have electricity, good sanitation, and to have time for oneself. For instance, now I have to spend a lot of my time—when I am not working—just in finding and preparing food for the family. There is no time for entertainment, or sports, or travel. It would be nice to have a TV satellite dish . . . or any of the things that are necessary for the enjoyment of modern life. The second reason I am depressed is that there is no possibility of a future for my children. My wife and I tutor them, but they still have to go to school for their accreditation. And the schools are very bad. My son, for instance, is in the eighth grade, and out of eleven subjects he has eight that have to do with religion or the Arabic language. It's very difficult for him—he is only twelve years old. All this started with the mujahideen.

"What I dream about for the future for Afghanistan is to have a stable government, to have electricity and paved roads, and good relations with our neighbors," Dr. Rostum said. "I hope that when the policy makers form their coalition they will not forget the educated people, the doctors and teachers and engineers who have been in Afghanistan during all these years of fighting. I say this because if Zahir Shah and his people come here from Europe to form a government and bring their aristocrats and their technocrats—they are of course welcome to include such qualified people—they should not forget those of us who were not with the Taliban or with the mujahideen. We have a right to have a voice in the future of our country."

From: Jon Lee 10/27/2001
I will be in the hotel room in Dushanbe waiting for your call. There is fog and sand everywhere today and suddenly it's freezing. Winter is definitely coming. I have managed to make arrangements to get to Istanbul on my existing ticket but need a new ticket for a flight to London. Can this be arranged?

From: Jon Lee 11/05/2001
The guy in London has given me a price for the Inmarsat phone that should solve our communication problems. 2,500 bucks. Have told him that I must sort out all the kinks by Wednesday.

From: Jon Lee 11/05/2001
I will need a cash advance, as you anticipate. Meanwhile, I hope to organize my expenses for the past trip tomorrow and send them off to you, but because of the overlap in what is going in and out I will need to know that cash to cover credit card bills and so forth is going into my New York account. I don't want to run low again, because out there it is well nigh impossible to get new funds quickly. Afghanistan and Tajikistan are both cash-only economies.

From: Jon Lee 11/06/2001
There may be a Tajik Air flight next Tuesday back to Dushanbe from Istanbul. If not, there may be a way to fly via Moscow.

From: Jon Lee 11/06/2001
Have placed an order for a new Thrane & Thrane Inmarsat, to be delivered in London tomorrow. Am making an appointment with computer/sat phone whiz to configure same when I pick up my new laptop. He will also reconfigure the Iridium and, hopefully, work out the kinks. I should be able to get back into Afghanistan by Thursday or Friday.

Re the laptop. It's a Panasonic Toughbook—a Pentium 3600 with a worldwide three-year guarantee and an extra-longlife battery (three and a half to five hours) and superduper casing (bulletproof).

From: Jon Lee 11/08/2001
Liza is trying to get me on the Moscow-Dushanbe flight on Monday, but there is a New Russia twist. There are no "legal" tickets, just unofficially obtainable ones. She will see the Tajik Air manager in the morning. Typical bloody thing, which means that I won't know if she's been successful until tomorrow. Just in case, she is seeing about flights out of Kazakhstan. (Tajik Air doesn't exist on normal flight-planning computers, so all of this requires major hassles.) In order to get a Kazakh transit visa (so I can get in the country and then get a Dushanbe flight) I need a letter from you stating who I am and that I will be leaving the country within seventy-two hours.

The Uzbeks were closed today but sound friendly. I will pop in tomorrow morning before I deal with the laptop.

From: Jon Lee 11/09/2001
It was one of those days. The laptop was delivered without the CD drive, and without the CD drive you can't configure the sat phones.

It is being delivered tomorrow. The Tajiks in Moscow have told Liza that they have taken note of my request to fly on Tuesday and will "process" it. This means she can't send me a confirmation of my onward flight, which means I can't fly to Moscow. She won't know what the dickhead Tajiks will decide until Monday.

From: Jon Lee 11/10/2001
Don't get too excited. This is just a test of the Toughbook. It's hooked up to the Internet. We are looking for the software for the Inmarset setup.

From: Thomas Dworzak 11/11/2001
To: Jon Lee
Things started rolling here a bit. A sort of offensive at the Kalakata/ Taloqan front line on the other side of the river. Managed to cross early in the morning with a few other journalists and got some stuff. Mamur Hassan led the attack. As of now the Northern Alliance lost all the positions they gained. Bad news: the translator, Nabi, defected definitely today. Did not like the shelling and wanted to go home for Ramadan. Sends you all his apologies. Conflicting reports that Taloqan has fallen to the Northern Alliance without a fight. So far no access in view from here. Taliban at the moment lobbing shitloads of shells in our direction. I heard that Uzbek-Afghan border still closed, but there are rumors that aid convoys will be going in in the near future. Am currently living in a donkey barn. Will be running low on film in a while. Not shooting too much digital, as it really gets on my balls. Hope you bring a bag for me stuffed with sausages and sweets.

From: Jon Lee 11/12/2001
Sharon: Seems that one of the three journalists killed last night was Volker, the Stern correspondent with Thomas. I heard early this morning from Heathcliffe that Thomas is OK. He is safe and

back in Dasht-i-Qala. I have no more details. Liza has a ticket for me from Moscow to Dushanbe on the Wednesday morning flight.

From: Liza Faktor 11/12/2001
To: Jon Lee
Thomas called at about 2 P.M. He has been carrying coffins all day. The Tajiks may be tougher on journalists moving around now, because of the deaths. I sent a fax to the Tajik press guy asking him to put you on the soonest convoy starting Thursday. There are also helicopters going now.

From: Jon Lee 11/12/2001
Sharon, I talked to Thomas. He is OK. Plans on going to Taloqan tomorrow. He agreed to keep me posted and not go too far ahead. Says Mamur will sort me out. Has been waiting for me and will help get me on a jeep going to Taloqan when I arrive.

From: Jon Lee 11/13/2001
It works!!! This is on the Inmarsat. It's working like a dream. We'll check the Iridium next.

From: Thomas Dworzak 11/14/2001
To: Jon Lee
Where should I go to meet up? Spent all day with Northern Alliance soldiers about thirty kilometers outside of Kunduz, at a place called Bangi. Still held by Taliban. Some casualties. As of now no link between Northern Alliance here and Dostum's forces. Kunduz is full of Taliban from all over. Northern Alliance apparently in negotiations with local Pashtun Taliban who want to change sides, but the "foreigners" (Chechens, Arabs, etc.) cannot surrender. Nothing very exciting going on news-wise. Population stoic about the whole thing, but they have bananas.

From: Jon Lee 11/14/2001
To: Thomas Dworzak
Am now in Dushanbe. My thinking is for you to stay there and let me catch up to you and maybe we do the story on that battle in Kunduz. Kabul seems too easy, and, as you point out, everyone is going there. It sounds like it will become a goatfuck. I will leave messages with Liza and on your French cell phone answering machine. OK?

From: Jon Lee 11/15/2001
To: Thomas Dworzak
Hiya. OK, this is what I am doing: driving to the border in a convoy, leaving seven A.M., Dushanbe. Arriving supposedly around two P.M. To save time and hassle can you please arrange to have a driver waiting? With your stuff and mine, I must have 80 kilos of gear. Have been trying to call you, but message says phone out of service.

From: Thomas Dworzak 11/15/2001
To: Jon Lee
Heavy U.S. bombardment on Talib positions outside Kunduz today. More Northern Alliance troops coming into town. Apparently fifty Taliban hiding in Taloqan discovered and arrested. General Daud, the commander here, claims that two planes from Pakistan evacuated the main Taliban from Kunduz last night.

Mamur Hassan's big buddy wants a bottle of Johnny Walker or any booze. He has a bookshop in town.

Some choppers flying around, but seems that convoy to river from Dushanbe and driving to Taloqan is the best way now.

I'm staying in a guest house on the fucking floor near "Kunduz Porte" on the main road. Left-hand side near city exit toward Kunduz. Usually get up around 0430 hours and am back around 1800, just after dark. Also might be in the only real restaurant coming from Dasht-i-Qala, to the left after the traffic circle, right-hand side. I always take all my stuff when I go toward Kunduz. As of now I have good contacts with the guys at a place called Kunduz Springs. There are a couple of big hay stacks on the left-hand side of the road. I might be there. Or they should know. It's about a forty-five-minute drive from Taloqan.

It shouldn't be a problem to hook up with someone on the border. There are lots of journalists in Taloqan. Hope trip goes well, and see you soon!! All best.

From: Jon Lee 11/15/2001
Sharon, so I guess I must literally look for Thomas in a haystack. Probably easier than it sounds.

From: Jon Lee 11/17/2001
Hey, this is on the Inmarsat with the Toughbook. I'm in Taloqan. Got your message. A Northern Alliance defense ministry official tells me that Americans are helping the Northern Alliance here pinpoint bombing targets and that they have been very effective. They expect to attack shortly.

From: Jon Lee 11/19/2001
Forget about sending me anything at that special e-mail address we set up. Suffice to say that Mr. London Computer Whiz fucked up bigtime. The system is working now, but only because Thomas managed to reconfigure it. Am thinking of sending a Taliban death squad to Mr. Whiz's house.

From: Jon Lee 11/19/2001
Four journalists were robbed and killed today after they were attacked while traveling on a bus from Jalalabad to Kabul. There were two incidents yesterday. One on the Jalalabad road, in which a group of journalists were robbed by bandits and sent back to Peshawar in

their underwear, but fortunately unharmed, and then the disappearance of a Reuters reporter on the outskirts of Kabul.

From: Jon Lee 11/23/2001
We hear that reporters waiting in Peshawar are pretty freaked out about traveling overland and that there is a long waiting list for flights to Kabul, which are going for $3,500 a head. A journalist here in Taloqan who was outside his house talking on his Iridium was shot at last night. They missed him, but it was a useful reminder that things are not entirely secure here, either.

From: Jon Lee 11/24/2001
Today I went to a nearby village to witness the surrender of several hundred Taliban. There were just as many mujahideen there, milling about, gesticulating and joking, their weapons wielded casually and haphazardly. One of the officers handed out masking tape and a poster of Massoud to paste on the windshields of vehicles.

As the convoy of Taliban began moving off toward Taloqan, escorted by mujahideen, I walked behind them, and several mujahideen approached me. One of them asked for a cigarette. I gave him one, but chided him, since it was Ramadan, and Muslims are not supposed to smoke during the daylight hours. Then another man came up and demanded a cigarette and I could see that the whole group of ten or so fighters were planning on doing this. So I said, No more.

A third mujahideen, a burly man with a large PK machine gun slung over his shoulder, leered at me and grabbed me between the legs, hard. Then he darted away and laughed. I followed him and kicked him in the rear end, twice. This made his comrades roar with laughter, but he didn't think it was so funny, and he pointed his gun at me, then lowered it. I began cursing him in English and he raised the gun at me again and I could tell that he was cursing me too, in Dari. We had something of a standoff.

I called for Yama, my translator, and asked him to tell me what the mujahideen was saying, but Yama, who was also arguing with the men now, refused to say. He did translate my threat to report the men to their commander, and he translated the burly man's response that he didn't give a shit, because he did whatever he wanted to do. I never was able to find someone in authority to complain to, and Yama just steered me away and muttered something about how war made people behave badly.

From: Jon Lee 11/26/2001
Was with the advance troops. Saw the fall of Kunduz. Very few other journalists. Mostly photographers. Shooting. Some sniping. A few iffy moments. Very beat. I tried writing and sending you more last night but was so tired I deleted it and couldn't bear to reconstruct. Will redo. Am running on about ninety minutes sleep but adrenaline makes up for the lack.

From: Jon Lee 11/27/2001
Sharon, I am having to do this in a hectic rush. Awoke this A.M. to news that during the night a gang of masked gunmen broke into one of the journalists' houses here in Taloqan and, after robbing and threatening them, shot a Swedish TV guy. Evidently he bled to death. By the time I was awoken, virtually all the press in Taloqan—BBC, CNN, and pretty much everyone else—was packing to evacuate in a mass convoy to Dasht-i-Qala and Dushanbe. It was not an option for us, I felt, since I still had reporting to do, and they were about to leave.

In the midst of all this, my friend Shahmurat arrived. I did our interview and then went to the house of a friend of his, a bookseller, who I wanted to interview also. Anyway, I am satisfied that we now have what we need. Returned here to find Thomas telling me that the Northern Alliance has declared all of Kunduz Province off limits to journalists. He said that CBS, Newsweek, and a few people who didn't take the convoy to Dasht-i-Qala have organized a convoy to Kabul. That seems our best, in fact only, option. In the last forty minutes (it is now noon and I felt it was too late, around three A.M. your time, to call you) I have packed everything up and we have paid our host. Our translator, Yama, has agreed to go to Kabul with us, and our one-legged driver (a mine casualty) too. We will leave tomorrow A.M. One or two journalists are missing, it seems. For tonight, Commander Daoud Khan will put everyone in an armed compound under his protection. Thomas is off organizing things while I write and send you what I have. I left you a message with the news about the journalist about 11:30 P.M. your time, but all this evacuation stuff has happened since. I will call you at the usual time and let you know what's going on.

The Surrender

A bdullah Gard lives in a run-down concrete-block house in Taloqan, a city of about two hundred thousand people in a fertile valley in northern Afghanistan. The headquarters of Ahmed Shah Massoud was in Taloqan until September 2000, when the Taliban captured the city. Abdullah Gard helped the Northern Alliance defend Taloqan, and when Massoud retreated, he went with him. But early this year Gard surprised many people who knew him by defecting, with his fighting force of several hundred men, to the Taliban. They fought against their former comrades-in-arms for months. Then, on November 11, as the Taliban abandoned one Afghan city after another, including Taloqan, Abdullah Gard and his men switched sides again.

I visited Abdullah Gard late one blustery afternoon a week after his most recent defection. Girls with brooms made of twigs were sweeping up autumn leaves under the plane trees outside his house. The gates in front of the house were guarded by a dozen turbaned fighters, and in the dusty yard children drew water from a well by hand. Several men escorted me into an upstairs room with red carpets on the floor and flat red cushions around the sides.

It was the third day of the Muslim holy month of Ramadan, about an hour before sunset prayers and the end of the day's fasting. A teakettle was set on a brazier in the corner, boiling water for the first tea to be drunk since sunrise. Through the window you could watch an American B-52 bomber flying slowly over Taloqan, trailed by double jet streams. The plane was on its way back from a bombing run over the nearby city of Kunduz, where thousands of Afghan, Chechen, Pakistani, Uzbek, and Arab fighters were still entrenched.

Abdullah Gard is a burly, bearded man in his late thirties. Three of his officers lounged around the room, staring at me, and one of them, a thin, gray-eyed man who played with plastic worry beads, glared suspiciously. Gard listened attentively as I explained my interest in understanding why he had switched sides twice in the war. Even one defection seemed anomalous to a Westerner, and the Afghans' acceptance of such things was puzzling. Gard replied that he was a special case, because—and this was the first time he had discussed this, he said—he had been acting secretly on orders from Massoud. He was a double agent. "I was to find out how many foreign troops there were here with the Taliban, their nationalities, who their commanders were, and their plans. And I was supposed to help Massoud from inside Taloqan when he launched an attack." Massoud was the only person who knew of the mission at first, but after Massoud was assassinated, a few others were brought into the picture. Most people still did not know why Abdullah Gard had switched sides.

Gard said that the majority of foreign troops in the north were "Punjabis," by which he meant Pakistanis; Uzbeks in the radical Islamic Movement of Uzbekistan, led by Juma Namangani; Arabs of various nationalities; and

Chechens. He said that they disagreed about strategy, although the common goal, of course, was the liberation of all of Afghanistan. But the Pakistanis argued that their country should be liberated next, and the Uzbeks insisted that it should be Uzbekistan. Not so long ago, Gard said, there was a rumor that Osama bin Laden had visited the north, but it was never confirmed, and he didn't see him.

Not all of the Taliban had been convinced by Gard's defection, and he was kept under surveillance. Once, he and his men were disarmed and he was told to stay in his home. During that period, he said, he refrained from contact with Massoud. Then, after a month, his command was returned to him. Just before the fall of Taloqan, he came under suspicion again. For most of his time with the Taliban, Gard said, he and his men operated as a mobile reserve battalion, and they were dispatched to places beyond Taloqan and Kunduz, such as Mazar-i-Sharif, Bamian, and Kabul.

I asked Gard how he had managed to persuade his fighters to go along with the ruse. He smiled. "That is my secret," he said affably. I pressed him. Surely, I said, he must have made an effort to avoid having his men on the forward lines, where they might kill his real allies? On the contrary, he replied. "I sent my men to the front line, and they were in some very bloody battles. Once, fifteen of them were captured, including five officers. One was taken prisoner and the other four were rearmed and returned to the battlefield as Northern Alliance fighters." Gard smiled, and shrugged. "They could not be told the truth, ever."

Gard said that he didn't particularly want to remain in the military. "If my country is secure, I would prefer not to continue being a commander." But how would he survive? "God is kind," he replied. "He will help us survive."

He had three wives, with whom he had had two sons and two daughters. Maybe he would have time to make more children. He laughed, and his officers laughed, too. It was sunset by then, and he left the room to pray.

IN THE FIRST WEEK of its liberation from Taliban control, Taloqan bustled and heaved with returning refugees and Northern Alliance fighters. Military vehicles, their horns blaring, careened around slow-moving donkey carts, darting children, and porters pulling handcarts loaded with goods. Jitneys drawn by horses adorned with ornamental red bobbles and jingling bells served as taxis. Occasionally, a helicopter clattered overhead, and several times a day B-52s added their dull roar to the din. Groups of boys hung out in front of newly opened kiosks where music blared and cassettes were sold. Under the Taliban, music was banned.

Taloqan is laid out in a geometrical grid of streets that are flanked by drainage ditches and lines of plane trees. Many houses are built of concrete rather than mud, and the main street is paved. The Taloqan River flows past the edge of town, and the land nearby is good for farming. Food stalls were stocked with fresh cauliflower, onions, radishes, red and yellow apples, pomegranates. Slaughtered lambs hung from meat hooks in butchers' stalls. There was plenty of the flat wheat bread, called naan, in the bakeries. The town has several *chaikhanas,* the traditional Afghan teahouses, where men gather to drink tea and eat kebab and rice with mutton. The *chaikhanas* provide space for sleeping, and at night large wooden platforms were filled with dozens of men lying willy-nilly alongside one another.

At the western end of town, the main street turns into the road to Kunduz, which lies forty miles away. The road snakes across a plain planted with wheat and dotted with small family farms. Mountains rise on all sides of the plain: a rumpled yellow, brown, and red anatomy of treeless hills ascend to great, snowcapped ridges. The new front line began at a bridge over a river near the village of Bangi, about twenty miles outside of Taloqan. The Taliban and the Northern Alliance were faced off at either end of a small valley, a half mile or so from each other. By mid-November, the fields were clipped stubble. As military trucks and tanks raced back and forth, children stood guard over husked wheat kernels that were spread out for drying in rectangular patches along the road.

One morning, I visited the military headquarters of Commander Daoud Khan, of the Northern Alliance, who was overseeing the reoccupation of Taloqan. There was a Toyota pickup truck smeared with mud outside the gate. Daoud's men told me that the truck had been driven across enemy lines and into town during the night by six Taliban field commanders who had defected, along with their three hundred fighters. I met two of the Taliban, dark men in disheveled black robes and turbans. They were surrounded by staring mujahideen. I asked one of the Taliban, who said his name was Muhammad Israel, why he had decided to defect, and he said that he had done so for the good of the country, in order to avoid unnecessary bloodshed. Given the fact that Kunduz was being bombed from the air and encircled by the Northern Alliance, I suggested, his decision appeared to have more to do with survival, but Israel pointed out that crossing Taliban lines with three hundred men, all of whom faced certain death if they were detected, had been very risky. He seemed to expect to be

commended for his bravery, and when I moved away he
and the other Taliban were regaling a group of mujahideen
with the details of their nocturnal adventure.

Commander Daoud, a former Massoud aide, is a tall,
strapping man in his late thirties. He said that since he had
taken control of Taloqan, thirty local Taliban commanders
had switched sides, bringing with them three thousand
men. He was hoping that more would follow. "I don't want
an attack to be launched on Kunduz," he said. "I want all
the Taliban in Kunduz to surrender and be taken captive."
He conceded that this was a faint prospect, given the large
number of foreign fighters in the city, most of whom were
thought to be ready to fight to the death. "If they don't
accept this, then we have no recourse but to push forward,
and to kill them."

DAOUD TOLD ME that the former Taliban commander in
Taloqan, Mullah Shabir Ahmed, was in "a safe location."
My translator, Yama, the twenty-four-year-old son of the
logistics chief for the Northern Alliance in this region, asked
around and discovered that the safe location was Daoud's
home, and he talked the guards there into letting us in. The
mullah, a rather pale, wan man in his mid-thirties, with a
long reddish beard, met me in an upstairs cubicle in a small
building just inside the front gate. He sat near the room's
sole window, an AK-47 assault rifle resting on the sill behind him. "I was studying at a madrasah in Pakistan," he said,
in a reedy, tired-sounding voice, "and when the Taliban
began I joined and entered Afghanistan with them, filled
with pure Islamic feeling. In the beginning, this feeling we
had was splendid, but, more recently, we have begun hav-

ing doubts about some of the commanders who are with the Taliban"—he was alluding to the bin Laden crowd of foreigners—"and, following the martyrdom of Ahmed Shah Massoud, we realized that outside hands, terrorists, were involved in the movement. So, for the good of the country, we decided to come over to the Northern Alliance." He and the two commanders under him—both men were in the room and nodded to me as he pointed them out—and several hundred fighters remained behind in Taloqan and turned themselves over to Daoud. The rest of the Taliban retreated to Kunduz. Shabir Ahmed said that he had stayed on to ensure the security of the town, and he had personally called Daoud to tell him that the way into Taloqan was safe. That was how Taloqan had been reconquered by the Northern Alliance.

Shabir Ahmed had not revised his Muslim beliefs. "I am still proud of the name Taliban," he said. "As for those incidents in the West"—the attacks on the World Trade Center and the Pentagon—"those were not the actions of the Taliban, but of terrorists. It's hurtful to hear the Taliban name insulted, and to see it used by others who have their own purposes in mind." He said that he didn't agree with all of the Taliban edicts, like the ban on kite flying and the prohibition of music, "but there are aspects of Sharia"—Islamic law—"which we do think are important, such as the rule against rape, pederasty, and fornication, against gambling and drinking alcohol. And also the importance of beards. These are things commanded by the messenger of Islam." He didn't think that all Muslims necessarily had to wear beards, and he opposed the destruction of the giant Buddhas at Bamian. "They posed no danger to Islam, and they were part of Afghanistan's history," he said. Mullah Shabir Ahmed spoke in a chantlike monotone that gave him, whether by intention or practice, a priestlike quality. He swayed back and forth slightly. I noticed that he had very clean, white manicured fingernails and toenails.

THE NORTHERN ALLIANCE MOBILIZATION for the advance on Kunduz began on November 22, Thanksgiving Day in the United States, amid conflicting rumors about negotiations for a surrender. Hundreds of mujahideen armed with rocket-propelled grenade launchers and Kalashnikovs began arriving in trucks and pickups at the Bangi front line. A large group of ethnic-Tajik Taliban had agreed to defect, and they were to rendezvous with representatives of the Northern Alliance at a village about a mile away. The sky was a deep and cloudless blue. A B-52 looped ponderously overhead, dropping bombs on the Taliban positions. B-52s are deceptively unthreatening. They drop their bombs while making banking curves, and there is a strange delay between the curves and the explosions, which appear to occur far from the bombers' flight path. On its third or fourth run, the B-52 dropped a tremendous bomb on the summit of a Taliban ridge—perhaps a thousand feet above the valley floor—sending a giant brown-gray cloud of dust and dirt cascading down the mountainside and eventually covering it, like an avalanche. Moments later, as the B-52 returned, men ran over the sides of the next Taliban ridge—which was still receiving tank fire—sending up their own dust clouds as they scrambled down the scree.

There was pandemonium at the Northern Alliance end of the valley, which looked like the scene of some kind of postmodern biblical theatrical event. Few officers appeared to be present, and mujahideen were swarming around aimlessly, their weapons pointing in all directions. Jeeps and trucks raced back and forth. Turbaned men wearing blankets had spiky antitank rockets sticking out like arrows from quivers on their backs. Others wore bandoliers of shiny brass bullets, which crisscrossed their torsos. There were flashes and booms from tanks and Katyusha rocket launchers and, in the foreground, wheat fields and a few flocks of longhaired black goats near the crumbling, fortresslike mud compounds of peasant farmers. Here and there, in random solitude, men knelt on their scarves, bending and rising in rhythmic prayer.

Sometime in the midafternoon, the mob of mujahideen began to scatter, cocking their weapons as they scrambled down the road. You could hear the sharp metallic clicks of their safeties snapping off. The men were screaming "Talib! Talib!" and some of them were pointing down the right side of the valley, where billowing dust clouds followed several pickup trucks headed in our direction. The trucks were carrying the defecting Taliban, and the panic subsided when the mujahideen realized that there was no hostile intent. Men who had run in the opposite direction came walking back, grinning as others teased them about their mistake. Within a few minutes, several of the pickups had roared across the bridge, and they came ripping through the crowd of mujahideen, who were still yelling "Talib," but smiling now. The Taliban were all armed to the teeth.

A big Russian Kamaz truck with a howitzer mounted on the back pulled up to great cheers. It was filled with Northern Alliance soldiers from the group that had gone to the rendezvous with the Taliban. (It turned out that during the rendezvous the defecting Taliban and the Northern Alliance greeting party had come under fire from more stalwart Taliban, and had had to run for it.) A few minutes later, the truck started off, heading toward Taloqan, and the mujahideen on the ground became angry. All of a sudden, I found myself standing alone in the road as the men on the truck pointed guns and half a dozen rocket-propelled grenades at the men who had been congratulating them and who were now screaming and pointing *their* guns. A battle seemed about to break out among the mujahideen over who was to take possession of the truck, and, indeed, as the truck pulled away, a soldier near me fired his gun, although the shot was high and in the air.

More pickups carrying Taliban appeared and parked on the road. I asked one young Talib, a husky youth in his early twenties dressed all in black, why he had defected, and he shrugged. "I came because my commander decided we should come," he said. He was from a province near the Tajik border, and he was looking forward to going home. When I asked him if he still considered himself a Talib, he said, "Yes, of course. I am a student of the Koran, and tomorrow I will still be a Talib. It is a holy thing to be."

Around three o'clock, the mujahideen began running or riding in trucks down the road toward several copses of trees that marked the Northern Alliance forward line. More tank, rocket, and machine-gun fire could be heard. Word trickled back that somewhere down there four Taliban had been killed. The B-52 bombed some more. The tanks on the ridges fired continuously, and after a while I could see that the Northern Alliance soldiers—their silhouettes clearly visible against the sky—had moved one ridge closer to the Taliban.

The Taliban commanders who had led the defecting troops were meeting with their Northern Alliance counterparts in a small room in a farmhouse. The room was dank and full of people; it reminded me of a photograph from the early days of the Russian Revolution. One of the two Taliban, a man with a red beard and a concerned expression, was talking to General Nazir, a senior Northern Alliance commander. Nazir was clicking worry beads and listening intently. The man was saying that the Taliban positions on the hill and in the valley ahead were very strong, and that the general should move his men out of their present positions and attack from the right side of the valley. The Taliban who were entrenched in the town of Khanabad, half way between Bangi and Kunduz, had eighty tanks and most of them were ready to resist to the death, he said. There were others who were willing to switch sides but had no one to help them. He advised Nazir to tell Commander Daoud that he should make contact with the Taliban commanders in Kunduz and Khanabad, and that many would defect if he could help arrange ways for them to do so. He criticized Nazir for the lax behavior of the mujahideen at the Bangi front line.

Back on the road, a scuffle was taking place between a mujahideen and a Talib. They were fighting over the Talib's jeep. I walked on, and about five minutes later I heard a bang, and once again people were running around and pointing their guns. Soon word came that a mujahideen had accidentally shot someone in the buttocks and grazed another man's head.

AS THE TALIBAN CONTINUED to defect during the next few days, I would often ask Yama, my translator, to identify the groups of fighters we saw near the Bangi front line. "Are they Talib or mujahideen?" There seemed to me to be precious little to distinguish them. Usually, the Taliban came across the front in vehicles covered in mud, to avoid detection from the air, but they wore virtually the same clothes as the mujahideen: pocketed vests, *patou* blankets, tunic and pantaloon outfits, a motley assortment of winter jackets, turbans, and scarves. They also carried the same weapons: Russian-made Kalashnikovs and antitank weapons. And they all drove Toyota pickups and Russian UAZ military jeeps and Kamaz trucks.

In general, the Taliban have fuller, longer beards than the mujahideen. The Taliban (though not all of them) wear black turbans, sometimes wrapped Tuareg style over their faces and necks against the wind and cold. Their commanders, who are often mullahs—although many of them are given the title simply out of respect—usually wear white turbans. The trademark headgear of the mujahideen is a flat-brimmed felt cap (brown, gray, beige, or white) called the *pakul,* which was worn by Massoud, and which became popular among the mujahideen during the anti-Soviet jihad of the nineteen-eighties. Not all mujahideen wear the *pakul,* however. Some merely wrap a striped or checked scarf over their heads or loop it around their necks. Or they wear a turban.

The Northern Alliance mujahideen are an unruly, noisy rabble much of the time, but the Taliban's fighters appear poised, watchful, and reserved. Those who defected to the Northern Alliance came in convoys, and at the handover points they usually stayed inside their vehicles, with the windows rolled up, or in the beds of trucks, sitting with their weapons next to piled-up gear. They would not speak, for the most part, unless given the OK to do so by a senior officer, and, when they did, they had an air of self-confidence. The mujahideen appeared to be in awe of them, and with good reason. Until the United States began making air strikes, the mujahideen were consistently defeated by the Taliban on the battlefield.

GHULAM SARWAR AKBARI OWNS A BOOKSTORE in Taloqan. He is a thin man in his early fifties with a pockmarked face and a gentle manner. He has large, intelligent eyes, and speaks some English, shyly. I met him in his house, a modest two-story building near a soccer field where military helicopters now take off and land throughout the day. Two of his grandchildren, both toddlers, played at his feet in the common room of the house. One of them has vision problems, and he wore adult eyeglasses that frequently slipped off his face.

Akbari grew up in Taloqan and went to a technical high school in Kabul, where he trained to become an air-traffic controller for the new Afghanistan that never came to be. He studied aviation and meteorology, and in the seventies, when the modernizing government of Muhammad Daoud was in power, he worked at different UN-sponsored weather stations around the country until returning to Taloqan, where he had a job at the airport. When the jihad against the Communist regime began, the airport and its facilities were destroyed. In the early eighties, the government of Babrak Karmal gave him the means to rebuild the weather station in Taloqan. This was a good time in his life, he says. "Government employees could survive on their salaries, and there were special coupon shops where we could buy things." Life continued in this fashion until the Soviet withdrawal from Afghanistan, in 1989, when Massoud's mujahideen took Taloqan. The new weather station was destroyed, and it was never rebuilt. Fearing for his life because of his affiliation with the Communist-backed government, Akbari fled with his family, along with the retreating government forces, to a village nearby. But the village fell to the mujahideen, and Akbari fled with his family again. In the early nineties, he moved to Kunduz, where he had a shop that sold items like shampoo and sugar and tea. When an amnesty was declared by the mujahideen government, he returned to Taloqan.

Akbari said that he had been a socialist, but that he didn't approve of many of the old government's ethnic policies, especially what he described as its partiality toward Pashtuns at the expense of other groups. Akbari is an Uzbek. "I believed, and still believe, that Afghan sovereignty should be preserved and the rights of all ethnic nationalities should be observed." I asked him whether he believed in the separation of church and state—a concept that is alien to most Afghans in the northern provinces—and he nodded.

Akbari described life in Taloqan under Massoud, when he first seized control, as difficult. "He seemed very strict; he tried to persuade people to pray and ordered women to wear Islamic coverings"—although not the burkha, which many rural women wore anyway. "Some people were imprisoned, and I felt in danger from Massoud's fighters. But this attitude became more moderate over time, especially after Najib"—President Najibullah, the Soviet-backed leader, who resigned in 1992—"was overthrown and the Islamic government decreed an amnesty." When the Taliban arrived in town, he was selling books of all kinds. His customers were most interested in history and fiction, he said, both foreign translations and books by Afghan and Iranian authors. Among their favorites were the works of Victor Hugo, Balzac, and John Reed, and books on politics and the military by the Najib-era Afghan general Azimi, as well as an Afghan history book by the late Mir Gholam Muhammad Ghobar, a classic.

"When the Taliban came to Taloqan, they always came to the shop," Akbari said, "looking for prohibited books, especially about politics and religion, and for any that might have images in them." He hid most of the books he thought they would find offensive. The only title they did confiscate, he says, was a songbook with the lyrics of the Afghan singer Ahmed Zahir. They didn't force him to sell religious books, but, since they were always asking for them, he and other booksellers tried to keep a good supply in stock. He gave me a look that said "Business is business." Now that the Taliban have left, he said, he has brought back out the books he'd hidden.

I asked him how he felt about seeing former Taliban walking, as it were, hand in hand with the Northern Alliance. What about the former Taliban commander of Taloqan, Mullah Shabir Ahmed? "I am at a loss about this merging of the two forces," he said. "Yesterday, Shabir Ahmed was a mullah wearing a turban and today he is living in Daoud Khan's house! And there are others who were wearing turbans and are now in *pakuls,* walking the streets." Akbari was appalled. "Every time a new government comes into power, the local strongmen change their disguises. They face up to no responsibility for the misfortune their wars cause to the civilians." He began to suggest that it was, as others had told me, the result of "foreign meddling." But Afghans were always blaming outsiders for their misfortunes, I said. He nodded, unperturbed. "Then it must be because of the poverty of the people. Need drives them to survive any way possible." A neighbor who had come in interjected, "It's all because of foreigners who want something from Afghanistan! Afghanistan is like a football kicked around between outsiders." Akbari concurred: "When there was fighting here between the government and the mujahideen, America helped the mujahideen in order to defeat the Soviets in Afghanistan. After the Soviets left, and the mujahideen were victorious, America, instead of helping them to create a good government, forgot about Afghanistan. America shouldn't have done this. It should have helped the mujahideen until there was a good government here. If that had been done, all this side-switching would never have happened."

ON SUNDAY, NOVEMBER 25, after the last large defection of Taliban troops, Commander Daoud Khan took a convoy part of the way up the valley toward Kunduz. We drove there early Monday morning, and around five o'clock began seeing mujahideen walking in the direction of Kunduz, large groups and small, as shambolic as usual. We drove around a big bomb crater with a smashed military vehicle at the bottom of it, and just before dawn, at a fringe of trees some four or five miles outside Kunduz, we caught up with the Northern Alliance army as it gathered for the advance on the city.

Abdullah Gard, the commander who had, on Massoud's orders, engineered a fake defection to the Taliban in order to gather intelligence, was coordinating the advance. He wore a *pakul* and green military fatigues with a gold-white-and-black scarf around his neck, and he carried a field radio. The Taliban were supposed to be moving to an area near the Kunduz airport, where they were to be disarmed and transported by General Dostum's forces to a fort near

Mazar-i-Sharif, a hundred miles to the west—although since many prisoners had already been killed in a battle at the fort the previous day, I wondered how cooperative the new group of prospective prisoners would be.

Abdullah Gard got out of his truck and began to walk, and so did we, sticking close to him. When the outskirts of the town were just visible across a low bridge, he climbed into a muddy graveyard, where the hummocks of graves were marked with flags on poles and metal placards with Koranic lettering, and listened to his radio. The front part of the convoy, mostly troops on foot, massed between open fields and walled family compounds. After about ten minutes, Gard walked back to the road and vanished with a large group of men. He had been asked to lead a flanking party toward a number of foreign Taliban who were believed to be hiding at the edge of the city. We were left with the soldiers on the main road, and, without any high-ranking commander in sight, we followed them as they crossed the low bridge and moved into the suburbs and toward the center of Kunduz. We were still moving on foot, with our jeep trailing behind.

There was some sporadic weapons fire and some rocket thumps, and soon we were in a more densely populated area, where civilians stood watching us pass. A mosque was at the end of the road, perhaps six blocks ahead. In a few minutes, word came down the line that a gun battle was taking place in the center of town, and cars began whizzing past us in wild retreat. Our driver was yelling for us to join the exodus, which we did, and then we ordered him to stop so that we could find out what had happened. We started and stopped two or three times over the next hour or so. About four blocks from the mosque, a man appeared in the center of the street, moving slowly

Northern Alliance soldiers on the road from Taloqan to Kunduz,
November 26, 2001

toward us, and as he passed I saw that he was covered with blood, and that one of his arms was loosely bound with an olive-green bandage. He held the injured arm with his good arm, and walked on, in a kind of determined trance, away from the center of town and whatever had happened there.

Around nine o'clock, Commander Daoud arrived from Taloqan with an entourage, and, as I waited to see him, I talked to friends of my translator, Yama, who is from Kunduz. They said that during the night there had been heavy bombing by American warplanes near the airport, and that there was a rumor that Pakistani planes had arrived, or tried to land, to evacuate Pakistani officers who were with the Taliban, and other foreign Taliban. Yama's friends spoke to one another in Dari, and I noticed that they used the English word "terrorist" (pronounced "tor-roh-riste"), which has evidently become part of the Afghan lexicon. No one knew whether the planes had been able to land or not, or what had happened, just as no one seemed to know what was happening in the city at that moment.

Someone told Yama that it was OK to go to the center of town, but when we got to the corner of the main street people were running, vehicles sped crazily past us, there was dust everywhere, and our driver beckoned frantically from the jeep, which was already moving. I climbed in, and once again we were leaving town without any clue about what was going on. Cars with fighters inside them roared by, but no one would stop. After about fifteen or twenty minutes, we began walking and driving back, and met a di-shevelled American journalist from the online magazine *Salon* who had been left behind by his driver. He said that there had been a fight between two rival Northern Alliance groups over Taliban cars.

In the bazaar area, several people were staring at the bodies of two Taliban fighters who lay dead in front of the shuttered shops. The bodies had been covered with robes, and people stopped to lift up the edges and peer at the corpses. The men had the gray, waxen look that even freshly dead people acquire. Blood coagulated in pools near their bodies. In one pool, a little plastic bag of *naswar,* the spicy chewing tobacco that most Afghan men use, sat upright. Farther on, next to another shuttered shop, a wounded Talib lay on his side in a dusty, bleeding heap. He looked sideways at passersby above his outstretched arm. No one was tending to him or seemed very interested in him, except for a man who explained that the wounded soldier was a "Kandahari," meaning a Pashto-speaking Afghan from the south.

A group of soldiers appeared, leading five young, dark-skinned Taliban captives, their arms tied behind their backs with their turbans. They were dirty and looked terrified. The soldiers seemed not to have decided what to do with them and, trailed by curious onlookers, they led them up and down the main street and finally took them into a carter's yard, where one of the soldiers shut the yard's high metal gates behind them. Along with some other journalists, I followed them, our idea being to prevent the soldiers from executing their prisoners. The young men were Pashtuns, they said, from Helmand Province, in southern Afghanistan, and just six weeks ago, a month before Ramadan, they had been forcibly conscripted and brought to Kunduz. They said that they didn't even know how to fight. Then, suddenly, their captors pushed them up some stairs and into a storage room. As we went up the stairs after them, the soldier who seemed to be in command stopped and said something to me in Dari. "He thinks

you are an American military man," Yama explained, "and
he wants you to give him a tip—*baksheesh*—because he
has captured these Taliban." After some explanation about
the difference between a journalist and a military man,
which seemed to puzzle the soldier, he let me pass.

The prisoners sat on their knees on a floor covered
with straw. The mujahideen who had asked me for a tip
stood over them and yelled, and the photographers took
pictures, and after a moment the soldier made everyone
leave but me and a woman photographer. I asked the men
why they hadn't surrendered, and they all answered at
once. Their commander had left them behind when the
shooting started, they said, and their comrades had run
away. They had hidden, and when they saw Northern Alliance soldiers approaching they gave themselves up and
handed over their weapons. The soldiers had cocked their
guns as if to shoot them, and then hit them with their gun
butts, and tied their arms behind their backs and led them
away. I told them that I would try to intercede with their
captors, who had by now disappeared.

There was a lot of activity on the street. Many ordinary people, men and youths, were walking around, smiling and giving the thumbs-up sign. A group of Northern
Alliance soldiers were taping posters of President Rabbani
and Massoud on a cement booth in the middle of a traffic
circle. An old man held aloft a poster of Massoud and yelled
"Down with Blind Mullah Omar, Long Live Massoud!" Just
then Commander Daoud drove up, and his car was surrounded by people, including the soldiers who had captured the five hapless Helmandi Talibs. The prisoners had
been taken out of the carter's storage room and were
being dragged around again. The man who had asked me
for a tip was talking to Daoud. Then he led the prisoners

away. I asked Yama, who had been within hearing range, what the soldier was saying. "He was asking Daoud for a tip because he had captured those men," Yama said. Yama led me half a block from the traffic circle, to a building with a hand-painted sign: "Let's Learn English: Kunduz English Language Centre: American and British Systems." It was his language school. He and his brothers ran it. They had hired several teachers in other subjects, like physics and mathematics, and it had become a kind of private high school, he explained. They had more than seven hundred students. We went back to the traffic circle, looking for our driver, and saw that the soldiers were still wandering around aimlessly with their prisoners. A little farther along the road, a man pushed a handcart containing the wounded Taliban from the storefront.

A LARGE NUMBER OF VEHICLES were parked beside a huge field that stretched away from the walls of a factory on the edge of town. A standoff was taking place, soldiers told us, with a group of a hundred or so armed Taliban. We walked along the lane between the field and the factory and saw several Taliban with machine guns, some of them pointed toward us, on the perimeter wall of a small mosque, and in the street just outside, facing them, several Northern Alliance soldiers. About ten minutes after we arrived, there was a tremendous explosion, apparently from an incoming anti-tank rocket, which landed somewhere behind us, followed by machine-gun fire. The shooting was coming not from the mosque but from a recess in the factory wall, where a man in a black turban was aiming a rocket launcher. We all ran around the corner and threw ourselves into a deep ditch.

The shooting, and more rocket explosions, continued for perhaps two minutes, and once or twice I popped my head up to see what was happening. All I could see was soldiers, lying prone or crouched in firing positions. Then it was quiet, and we left the ditch to take shelter behind the thick pillar of a house.

We took a circuitous route away from the factory, which was now cordoned off by soldiers, and drove to Yama's house, a compound in a pleasant working-class suburb of the city, with a well, a cookhouse, a mud-walled toilet, and a cow tethered in the yard. His brothers and cousins and little sisters (I never saw his mother, because it would have been inappropriate for her to appear before a strange man) welcomed him home, and, in spite of Ramadan, we were served a lunch of fried eggs and vegetables.

That afternoon, back in Taloqan, I looked up a man named Shahmurat, whom I had met several weeks earlier, when the American air campaign in Afghanistan began. Shahmurat is a big, irreverent man in his early fifties. He is the son of a relatively well off rural landowner (two hundred acres of land and some livestock) and the respected elder of his home village. Shahmurat studied at an agricultural school in Kabul, and when he returned home, as he tells it, he was unanimously named the *arbob,* or headman, of his village. He was *arbob* for six years. "My job was to make peace, and to be the intermediary between the government and the people," he explained. He did this until the Communist regime that overthrew President Daoud came to power and the rural Afghan feudal system—and, with it, his job—was abolished. He remembers those years, the waning years of Zahir Shah's monarchy and Daoud's brief stint in power, as a good time. "There was a government that the people respected," he said, "and no one complained about economic problems. There was peace."

Shahmurat was among those who opposed the new regime and the changes it brought. "Enlightened people gathered together and took up arms against the Communist government, and began to fight," he said. He eventually signed on with the Jamiat-i-Islami organization headed by Burhanuddin Rabbani and Ahmed Shah Massoud. He fought with Jamiat against the Communists for five years, until one day he had a change of heart.

"After five years, I realized that this war was meaningless to me, that East and West were both involved in Afghanistan for their own designs. I cashiered my troops, gave my weapons to other commanders, and returned to my family in my village." I asked whether something specific had happened to make him do this. "Our enemy was the Soviet invader," he explained. "But the mujahideen ended up fighting between themselves. So I went home. That was in 1983." He was also fed up, he said, with the increasingly radical Muslim character of the mujahideen organizations. "When they caught a government soldier, they killed him, and I disagreed with this practice. This was because of their fanaticism." Islam was supposed to preach tolerance and respect, he said. "The mujahideen became more and more fanatical during the war against the Soviets, and they remained so afterward, when they came to power. But they were powerless when they took over the government, because they fought with one another. And then came the Taliban."

From 1983 until a few weeks ago, Shahmurat stayed at home in his village, tending his family farm, and living simply. It was the drought of the past three years that had brought him to Taloqan, where he hoped to find work.

What did he hope to do? I asked. He shrugged. "Anything," he said. "Now there is no work. The whole country is poor. The money is all with the powerful commanders." Shahmurat seemed pessimistic and woeful.

I asked him to explain all the switching of sides that we had been witnessing recently. Why did Afghans change allegiances so easily? "In America and other places," Shahmurat said, tentatively, "people have the idea that their countries are important to them. But in Afghanistan the fighters don't have this notion, and the poverty here leads them to join whoever is powerful." Shahmurat, like Ghulam Sarwar Akbari, who is his friend, blamed the foreign powers that had armed and backed various Afghan factions. "These armed organizations have been supported by foreign countries who don't care whether Afghans are educated or not, and they have pushed the fighting men to kill the educated people and those with culture. And so now there are no educated, cultured people anymore. They are either dead or in exile, and if they are still in Afghanistan they are in their homes, and have no power to speak. The gun now governs Afghanistan. In other countries, the security of the people and the property of the nation is guaranteed, and this is also so within Islam. But here these things have been destroyed. How can we change this?" Shahmurat said that he hoped for a UN-sponsored political solution in Afghanistan. "Perhaps, through the UN, enlightened people can come to power in Afghanistan. When a person is thirsty, he wants water. Afghans are thirsty for unity and peace. We are sick of war."

From: Jon Lee 12/01/2001

Arrived in Kabul tonight (Saturday) five minutes before curfew. Thomas and I are on the floor of a room in the Hotel Spinzar that is shared by Julius Strauss and a photographer. Funky, but it has electricity.

Our convoy from Taloqan was made up of twelve journalists of various nationalities—Britons, Poles, Germans, French, an Israeli, and me, the only American—and a battery of Afghan drivers, translators, and four Northern Alliance soliders who were paid to come along as security. After forty minutes of paved road we set out overland, and, for four days, at an average speed of eight miles an hour, journeyed fitfully south, driving along riverbeds and rocky tracks that led us over the Hindu Kush.

Just before dusk on the afternoon of the second day, we came to a town that is notorious for its bandits. We halted briefly and didn't get out of our vehicles. Enam, our driver, whispered to me that last year he had been part of a large convoy of trucks carrying goods that had stopped there and that he had overhead men in the bazaar discussing how they would rob and kill everyone if they stayed the night. About an hour later, Enam flipped the jeep onto its side while trying to negotiate an uneven stretch of road. No one was hurt, but the jeep was battered. We managed to heave it upright and got it started again and continued through the night, but were soon stopped by five men who appeared suddenly in the headlights. Their leader had a gray beard and wore a turban and a patou blanket and carried an AK-47 assault rifle. Four younger gunmen stood beside our vehicles while the older man had an argument with the forward contingent of guards, who were in a pickup just in front of our car. Suddenly the soldiers roared off, leaving us behind, and the lead gunman came over to us. He was shouting and yanked open the front door of the jeep and pressed his weapon across the lap of Yama, my translator. He yelled something in Dari, and Yama yelled back. The gunman slammed Yama's door and yanked open the one next to me. He poked his head in and glared, then slammed my door and strode away, making angry noises. We told Enam to drive off.

Yama said that the man with the AK-47 had been demanding a ride for himself and his four companions, but that they were surely bandits and would have robbed us. We caught up with the soldiers and a few cars that had gone ahead of us, and waited anxiously for the rest of the convoy. There were gunshots behind us. A few minutes later the other cars appeared, and we were told that the bandits and the second security detail had been ready to shoot it out, but that one of the soldiers had talked the bandits down, arguing, among other things, that if anything bad happened to the foreigners (i.e., us), other foreigners would come to take revenge. While the bandits were chewing this over, a party of local gunmen affiliated with the Northern Alliance appeared out of the night, fortuitously, and the bandits decided to back off.

An hour or so later, the driver of one of the other jeeps, which was carrying two British journalists, lost control of his brakes as he went up a steep hill. The jeep rolled over five or six times and came to halt upside down, pinning one of the Brits' arms underneath it. Nobody was killed or, it seemed, badly hurt, but the reporters were shaken up and cut and bruised, and the man whose arm had been injured was in a good deal of pain. The smashed-up jeep was left in a nearby village, and arrangements were made for the injured men to stay in a mosque while the convoy went on to get help for them. Then, at the last minute, the village mullah changed his mind. Evening prayers were going to be held in the mosque, and the journalists would be in the way. So we piled the injured men into other cars and continued on our way.

That night we stayed in a tiny mountain chaikhana, teahouse, and spent the next day in the snow, alternately walking and pushing the jeeps over the Khawak Pass, the last major obstacle before we entered the Panjshir Valley.

City of Dreams

T he tomb of Ahmed Shah Massoud is in a shallow cave burrowed into a hill in the Panjshir Valley. The grave site, which is near the edge of a crude road cut along the steep valley slopes, is marked by a green sign with hand lettering that spells out "Chief of the Martyr's Hill" in Farsi and in English. The Panjshir Valley—a canyon some hundred and twenty miles long, stretching southwest from northern Afghanistan to the Shamali plain, just north of Kabul—is a bleakly rugged place. The road often falls away or is narrowed by mud slides, and ruined Soviet-era military tanks and armored personnel carriers litter the route, along with the twisted carcasses of trucks and jeeps that have slipped off the road onto the rocks below.

Massoud was born in Bazarak, a village less than a mile up the Panjshir River from Martyr's Hill. He was a national hero long before he was murdered, on September 9th, and he has since become a figure of quasi-religious dimensions. Travelling down the valley toward Kabul at the beginning of December with several other journalists, I noticed that my driver, Enam, who is a native Panjshiri, had tied a black flag of mourning to the antenna of our jeep. There was a

107

Massoud poster plastered to the windshield, practically obscuring it, and a small photograph of Massoud taped onto the driver's-side window. We were part of a convoy of seventeen vehicles, many of which were decorated in a similar fashion.

It had taken us four days to travel about two hundred and fifty miles—south from the city of Taloqan, over the Hindu Kush, and into the Panjshir Valley—across an isolated, edgy region where the Northern Alliance seemed to have only a tenuous presence. On the fourth day, the sun was setting on Massoud's grave as we made our way toward the paved road that crosses the plain to Kabul. Once we were on the road, our headlights illuminated blasted vehicles, ruined tanks, collapsed houses, and broken walls covered with starbursts from shell fire and pocked by bullets. After the Taliban took Kabul, in 1996, they destroyed all the villages in the Shamali, emptying the area of civilians and creating a buffer zone for their front line with the Northern Alliance, which forayed out from the Panjshir. In the weeks leading up to the Taliban's retreat from Kabul, in mid-November, the frontline positions had been heavily pounded by American bombers and warplanes, and the road was gouged and cratered. Enam drove slowly and weaved around the holes, but was careful not to get too close to the edge of the road. Newly posted signs warned of land mines.

Kabul appeared out of the night, shockingly, as we reached the top of a small cluster of hills that rose from the plain. There was light everywhere. Glowing squares and rectangles of white, blue, and yellow crossed the valley. It was the first Afghan city I had seen with a functioning electrical system.

* * *

WITH THE TALIBAN GONE, Kabul has reverted to being the one city in Afghanistan where, in relative terms, almost anything goes. Liquor is still forbidden and scarce, but it's available. Street vendors sell postcards of sultry Indian screen idols, and cockfights have resumed. Metalworkers are doing a brisk business in satellite dishes, which are hand-beaten from scrap; the finished products are covered with the logos and brand names of canned goods, making them look like pop art. The cult of Massoud is also flourishing. Throngs of young men scuffled for tickets to the premiere of a French documentary, *Massoud l'Afghan,* and an official morning of homage was held recently at several of Kabul's main mosques. Northern Alliance soldiers laden with Massoud posters tucked them under the windshield wipers of cars, like parking tickets.

Yet there seems to be an underlying uncertainty about the changes that have taken place so suddenly. A British reporter and I were walking around downtown one morning, and we stopped on a street where there were several washing-machine and appliance-repair shops. My companion decided to interview a twelve-year-old boy who was working as a repairman. A group of curious men and boys soon surrounded us, and I noticed that four women in blue burkhas had paused to watch as well, from a short distance away. After a few minutes, the women came forward, and one of them, who said her name was Shahkoko and that she was forty-five years old, asked if we knew of any foreign aid agencies or NGOs that needed English-speaking Afghan personnel. She had once been a teacher, she said, and under the Taliban had continued teaching, clandestinely, in her home, to help her family survive. But she had been discovered, and the Taliban had detained her teenage son, beaten him, and cut him with knives. So she had stopped giving her illegal classes. Now she was desperate to find real, paying work again. I took down her name, and two men who were listening helped me sort out some confusion over her street address.

Suddenly, we were interrupted by an irascible bearded man who owned one of the shops. He yelled at Yama, my translator, who is from northern Afghanistan. The bearded man was a Pashtun—a member of the tribal group that most of the Taliban are also from—and he excoriated Yama for helping foreigners talk to Afghan women. Yama was a yokel from Badakhshan Province, he said, which was an insulting reference to Yama's Tajik heritage. This upset Yama, who tried to pull me away, but by then I was angry, and I cursed the man and called him a "Talib." Shahkoko, the former teacher, nodded her head vigorously. "Thank you," she whispered. "You are right, he is a Talib." Then she and her friends moved quickly down the street, away from us and the little mob scene. My companions and I went in the opposite direction, leaving the shopkeeper blustering on the pavement. Yama chastised me for my outburst. "You cannot talk this way in Kabul yet," he said. "It is not safe for you. There are still many people here who think like the Taliban do."

It must be strange for many of the citizens of Kabul to be dealing with Western expectations when until only a few weeks ago the only foreigners in the city—or in the country, for that matter—were the Pakistanis, Chechens, Uzbeks, and Arabs fighting alongside the Taliban and Osama bin Laden's Al Qaeda organization. They have all vanished, and in their place are several hundred journalists from all over the world, who have packed the city's few hotels, rented scores of cars, and hired numerous translators. On the curb outside the Herat Restaurant, a kebab-and-pilaf place whose walls are adorned with old black-and-white photographs of Afghanistan's principal ancient sites (except for the destroyed Bamian Buddhas, which are curiously absent, as if they had never existed), a contingent of beggar boys and women in dirty burkhas are on permanent stakeout. The Herat is said to have been the favorite dining spot of the foreign Taliban in the capital, before the journalists came.

In the residential district of Wazir Akbar Khan, where carefully laid out tree-lined streets and public parks recall a time when Kabul was almost a modern city, workmen are busy repainting and restoring dilapidated houses for media organizations. There is a *Newsweek* house, a *New York Times* house, and an ABC and CBS house. A British journalist who is setting up a Kabul office for his television news agency has rented a house in which one of Osama bin Laden's wives used to live. The United Nations has resumed its operations, as have a number of international relief agencies, and foreign embassies are reopening. The Russians, British, Iranians, Turks, French, and Germans were among the first to come back, and in mid-December a group of American marines went into the U.S. embassy compound, which had been closed since 1989. The marines swept the grounds for unexploded ordnance and set up machine-gun nests behind sandbags on the roof.

A single concrete office tower rises some eighteen stories above the city center. It is the Telecommunications Ministry, Kabul's tallest building, and perhaps the last vestige of the days when Afghanistan seemed to have some kind of future. Architecturally, it is as though time had stopped in Kabul in the late seventies. Nothing much appears to have been constructed since then, except for dingy Soviet-built apartment blocks, and one half-finished bank building and a mosque, both begun under the Taliban.

A GREAT DEAL HAS BEEN DESTROYED. One day while I was driving around the city with Fridoun, an affable twenty-three-year-old medical student, I remarked that he was born just about the time that the war against the Communists began —the jihad that was followed by civil war. "Yes," he said. "All I know is war. For me, rockets and bombings—all these things are normal." He shrugged. He was eager for Kabul's medical school to reopen, so that he could finish his studies and become a doctor. As we drove along the Kabul River, which has for several years been nearly bone-dry because of a drought, and began to circle the city, the scale of the destruction was overwhelming. Entire sections of Kabul have been obliterated. Block after block of buildings is a dismal ruin of bricks and twisted concrete; roofs have caved in, façades are full of bullet holes or have been pierced by tank shells. Fridoun explained what had caused each piece of devastation, and after a while it seemed as though we were examining the city the way one assesses the age of a dead tree by counting the rings in its stump.

Fridoun pointed out the beat-up tomb of King Nadir Shah—the father of Zahir Shah, who is now in exile in Rome —on a large dirt hill not far away. The hill was honeycombed with abandoned dugouts and fortifications, and sparsely adorned with martyrs' flags. It had been one of the front lines in the fighting over Kabul that began in 1992, when President Burhanuddin Rabbani and Massoud took power. The ruined buildings, lone walls, and solitary columns below the hill resembled giant sand castles or sections of an archaeological dig. "This area used to be very famous as a place of business for people coming in from the provinces," Fridoun said. "There were many hotels and shops." Now several ragged men and children were selling scrap metal and recycled spare parts for cars; bicycle repairmen sat on boxes at the roadside next to inner tubes, waiting for customers.

Fridoun said that Gulbuddin Hekmatyar, a Pashtun Muslim fundamentalist backed by Pakistan and Saudi Arabia (and, during the anti-Soviet jihad in the nineteen-eighties, by the CIA), had established a base in the mountains fringing the city beyond the hill, and from there he was able to rain rockets on the population, which he did with vicious abandon—even though he was officially the prime minister of the mujahideen government during this period. Massoud was at first assisted in the defense of the city by the Uzbek warlord Abdul Rashid Dostum, who had fought with the Soviets against the mujahideen until 1992, when he switched sides, thereby facilitating Massoud's seizure of Kabul. Dostum switched sides again in 1994. From the same hill where he had fought with Massoud against Hekmatyar, Dostum now turned his guns against Massoud. Then the Taliban attacked Hekmatyar and Dostum from behind. They retreated, and Massoud faced the Taliban and another mujahideen faction, the Hazara—ethnic Shias—who were entrenched in western Kabul, around the university. "What people say," Fridoun explained, "is that Massoud told the Taliban, 'Let's join together and finish the Hazara.' " In any case, he said, the Taliban began fighting with the Hazara, killed their leader, and Massoud chased them out of the city. "Then," Fridoun continued, "Massoud attacked the Taliban."

Southern Kabul in the winter of 2001

Fridoun went on in this manner as we drove into the devastated western suburbs, and I stopped trying to keep track of the precise chronology of what destruction was caused when and by whom. The result, in the end, was the same. All of the devastation had a name attached to it, and most of the names were still key figures in Afghanistan's politics. As we passed the former Soviet Cultural Center, Fridoun pointed across the road to a large building that had been peppered by gunfire. "This was where the Hazara killed their prisoners when they were in control here. They killed them by shooting, by *halal,* as we say"—Fridoun drew an imaginary knife across his throat—"by fire, by boiling water, and even by driving nails into heads."

I asked Fridoun how he felt about showing me the ruins. "I feel ashamed," he replied. "I feel ashamed that a foreign person sees this and thinks: This was destroyed by Afghans themselves." Then what did he think about the men who had done this, men who were still wielding power? "We know this is their last chance to be here with guns," he said softly. "If there are elections in Afghanistan for a new government, none of these people will be voted for. The people are very angry with these men. Right now, I know, if I say 'Massoud is bad' in Kabul, I will go to prison. But if democracy comes I can say who is bad and who is good, and I can vote for whoever I want to lead Afghanistan."

PROFESSOR MUHAMMAD KAZEM AHUNG is a writer and intellectual who stayed in the city during most of the years of turmoil. He received me in his home, a drab, two-story concrete-and-glass house with a walled garden. It must have been a comfortable, upper-middle-class residence once, but now it was freezing cold inside, and there seemed to be no furniture. Ahung apologized for this, indicating that I should sit on some cushions arranged around a frayed carpet. There was nothing on the walls of the house, either upstairs or downstairs. It seemed to have been stripped bare except for the floor coverings.

Professor Ahung is a robust man of sixty-eight, but—unusual for an Afghan—he appears younger. He has a neatly trimmed salt-and-pepper beard, and on the day we met he was wearing a woollen waistcoat over a traditional Afghan long shirt and pantaloons. He speaks excellent English, and since he was clearly uncomfortable in the presence of the translator I had brought—a young Panjshiri named Qias, who has relatives who are officers in the Northern Alliance—I asked Qias to go to the bazaar to buy some fruit. Professor Ahung relaxed and brought me tea and biscuits, even though he was observing Ramadan.

Ahung grew up on a farm on the Shamali plain, where his father, who was an army officer, had retired to live on the land and grow grapes. He went to Kabul University and graduated from the Academy of Letters in 1958, then began working in the Ministry of Information and Culture. He became chief of the reporting staff of the government's official daily gazette, and in 1963 he went to East Lansing, Michigan, where he earned an M.A. in journalism at Michigan State. When he returned to Kabul, he was promoted to assistant chief editor, but in 1966 he was fired, he says, because he had been accused of being a member of the Afghan Communist Party. "I am a socialist by inclination, not an extremist," Ahung said. "Not like these people"—he motioned to the world outside the windows of his house. He spoke with warmth of his two years in the United States, and of the time immediately afterward, back home in Kabul, when he was an avid visitor at the United States Information Service library. "In those days, the Western press was very well represented here," he said. "The library had copies of *Time, Life, Ladies' Home Journal,* the *London Illustrated News.* We read everything, and I translated many articles for Afghan readers."

Ahung continued to work as a writer for the Ministry of Information, and he also began teaching journalism classes at Kabul University: "I taught reporting, and English as a second language, a course designed for journalists." In 1973, the king was overthrown in a bloodless coup by his cousin, Muhammad Daoud, and five years later Daoud was killed by Marxist military officers and replaced by Nur Muhammad Taraki. At this point, Ahung's journalistic career took off again. "Since I had some really close personal friends who were involved in the revolution," he said, "they proposed to Taraki that I become head of the *Kabul Times.*" Taraki agreed, and Ahung stayed on as editor when Taraki was executed by Hafizullah Amin, his deputy. Amin was murdered soon afterward, and Babrak Karmal, the leader of a rival Communist faction, became president.

Babrak Karmal came to power in 1979, when the Soviets invaded Afghanistan, and he fired Ahung from the *Kabul Times.* Ahung retreated, once again, to Kabul University, where he taught and wrote articles and books. He was the dean of the journalism school for twelve years. He had written more than twenty books, he said, although most were no longer in print. He remained at the university until the Taliban purged the school of those who were not appropriately Islamicized. Since then, he had tried to keep busy. He had even written a number of short stories. He showed me a book that was published this year in Pakistan. I barely recognized him in the photograph on the jacket. He had a long beard, grown to appease the Taliban. I asked Ahung what had kept him going. "I'll tell you," he said. "Whenever the regime in power thought I felt this way or that, contrary to their way of thinking, they usually just fired me and I went home and said nothing. I shut up. I became a conservative! That is how I survived." Hadn't this self-censorship been difficult? I asked him. He pondered a moment. "Well, no," he said. "If I had shouted, they would have put me in jail, and what would have been the use of that? If I was ousted from my country, what could I do? Who could I help in places where the people are better educated than myself? I could have gone to Iran or Pakistan, but the Iranians look down on Afghans for reasons of language and culture. And the Pakistanis, they are businessmen, in every sense of the word—you know what I mean."

Ahung blames the Communists for having begun the destruction of Afghanistan. "Before, economically and culturally, and in terms of social equality, we were making progress. But this was destroyed by the Communists. I was among them, but I did not want that."

Ahung seemed to have few illusions about his pragmatism and its costs. "Spiritually and intellectually, I did not feel particularly proud about things," he said. "Materially, I was just able to sustain myself and my family. Meanwhile, I encouraged others not to be conservative like me. I encouraged them, my students and my sons, to fight for their beliefs. But I had students who spied upon me. They have called me treacherous," he said indignantly. "They have."

Professor Ahung and his wife live alone in the house in Kabul. "I'm getting old," he said. "I have five sons and three daughters and twenty-four grandchildren. They are all independent and live away from here." His three daughters are married and live in Herat with their husbands. Three of his five sons went to the former Soviet Union to study and have not returned. A fourth son followed them there, and the fifth works for an international relief agency in Herat. Ahung's wife—whom I never saw, although I heard her rustling around in an adjacent room occasionally—missed the children, and he tried not to be away from the house for long, so that she wouldn't be alone. "Of course I feel sorrow," he said. "But what I do is I sit with myself, and I say, 'Throw it out of your mind.' And it works, you know, it goes." He had not yet been asked to resume his duties when the university reopens next spring. "With all due respect," he said, "I am not going to ask. I am not going to sacrifice my pride. I have no money. I have sold all of my carpets, my dishes, and my wife's gold in order to survive these past six years. My house and farm in Shamali, which used to give us some small income, was burned down. They should come to see me, for my pride."

I asked Ahung how he felt about things now, with the Taliban gone and political change in the air. "I am disturbed," he said. The previous evening he had listened to the fundamentalist mujahideen leader Abdul Rasul Sayyaf speak at a nearby mosque. The Afghan delegates who had met in Bonn to establish an interim government in Kabul had just announced who would be in the new administration, and Sayyaf and other conservative Afghan leaders were angry at not being given posts. "Sayyaf said that if the U.S.-supported interim government came and the king returned, guerrilla war would begin again in Afghanistan," Professor Ahung said. "This disturbs me."

The Bonn agreement was a victory for the Massoud loyalists. Muhammad Fahim, who became the Northern

Alliance's defense minister after Massoud's assassination, kept his job in the new government, as did Massoud's close friend Abdullah Abdullah, the foreign minister, and Yunis Qanouni, the interior minister. All of them, like Massoud, grew up in the Panjshir Valley. President Rabbani, who is an ethnic Tajik from a northeastern province, had to relinquish his office to Hamid Karzai, a Pashtun from a prominent family in Kandahar. In a few months, a Loya Jirga, a traditional assembly of various Afghan groups, was to meet and choose a more permanent government. "We all know that if the U.S. had not bombed this country looking for Osama bin Laden," Professor Ahung said, "we would not have an interim government. As an American, you should feel responsible for this whole thing, and for Afghanistan, because if you leave there will be a civil war, and it will be worse than ever before."

THE AFGHAN PRESIDENTIAL PALACE is in the sprawling, park-like nineteenth-century royal compound in downtown Kabul. The grounds of the complex are unkempt now, and the roofs of several buildings have caved in, apparently because they were hit by rockets, or perhaps tank fire. I went there to speak to President Rabbani's eldest son, Salahuddin, whom I had met several weeks earlier in Faizabad. He had accompanied his father to Kabul when the Taliban left. I waited for Salahuddin in a room that had a huge gray metal Soviet-era intercom system clumsily inscribed with Cyrillic lettering. It clashed with the crystal chandelier, heavy curtains, Persian carpets, and gilded furniture. Salahuddin greeted me in the private presidential meeting room. It was the first time, he said, he had talked to someone there, and he seemed to be enjoying himself. The room was dark and cold, but there was a small, Russian-made electric heater in the corner that made it bearable.

Salahuddin said that he had not been back to London since September, and that he hoped his family would join him in Afghanistan, perhaps next summer. He was diplomatic about the new government and about his father's position. "I'd say that my father is not angry," he said, "but that he is not entirely happy, either." They approved of Hamid Karzai as the new leader, but would have liked what Salahuddin described as broader representation for other members of the Northern Alliance. He shrugged and smiled. "I think there was pressure for a quick fix in Afghanistan, and you know that no such thing is possible here."

I asked Salahuddin what he thought was going to happen. "All I can tell you is that my father is ready to hand over power," he said. "But as for the rest I cannot say." A Northern Alliance security official who had been close to Massoud had told me privately that the day after the Bonn agreement was announced, General Fahim became so angry about Rabbani's complaints that he threatened to arrest him. Fahim backed down, but he told Rabbani to stay in his residence and to shut up. Fahim had also issued some kind of ultimatum to General Dostum, and, coincidentally or not, several days later Dostum told reporters that he had no intention of spilling blood over his differences with the new government.

Salahuddin said he had hoped that the UN would not attempt to impose a disarmament process, and in fact that possibility had been left out of the final text of the Bonn agreement. "What do you think," Salahuddin said, "that the Blue Helmets would be able to come and say to the people,

'Give me your gun'? The gun is more than about power and survival; to Afghans having a gun is a source of pride. You can't just take them away. So this is impossible in Afghanistan." He had also been troubled by the preliminary language for one of the clauses of the agreement, which he described as calling for justice against perpetrators of past atrocities. "This is a real problem," he said. "How to define atrocities. There are many commanders who have killed people who might fear that they could now be considered war criminals. Our soldiers have killed a lot of Taliban. Does that constitute an atrocity?" This argument prevailed in Bonn, and the final version of the pact didn't address retribution.

After we had chatted awhile, Salahuddin said, rather abruptly, "Now I have a question for you. What is your opinion of my prospects for a political future here in Afghanistan?" In Faizabad, people had referred to Salahuddin —although not in his presence—as "the Vice President," and I had once told him so. He had laughed then, and looked pleased. Now it was less of a joke.

I told Salahuddin that I thought that Afghanistan's older generation of political leaders had failed abysmally, and that his country needed the ideas of a new generation of people who were educated and knowledgeable about the modern world but were also in touch with their own culture.

"That is what I have been thinking, too," Salahuddin said.

As he was showing me out, Salahuddin introduced me to the palace's oldest employee, a bearded man in his late sixties who wore a coat with shiny buttons and who stood at attention as we passed. He had been at the palace since the time of King Zahir Shah, Salahuddin said, although he had been dismissed by the Taliban. The Rabbanis had asked him to return. He and Salahuddin bantered about presidential secrets, and Salahuddin described one of the important events that the old retainer had witnessed: the moment in 1959 when Queen Homaira, King Zahir Shah's wife and the leader of a movement to liberate modern Afghan women, threw off her veil. The old man nodded, confirming this, but kept silent.

From: Jon Lee 12/10/2001
Julius Strauss left Kabul for Jalalabad with three companions and seven armed bodyguards in a hired minibus. The next morning, he called to say that they had arrived, but only after a terrifying encounter with a group of men who had leapt out in front of their vehicle, aiming rocket-propelled grenade launchers and Kalashnikovs at them. Their bodyguards drew their weapons, causing the attackers to pause, and the driver gunned the accelerator and they escaped.

From: Jon Lee 12/15/2001
It now seems that there will be no convoys from Kabul to Jalalabad until the 19th or even 20th, after the post-Ramadan festival of Eid. There was a convoy organized by NBC today—not tomorrow, as we'd thought—and we packed and rushed and tried but failed to get on. Met a Der Spiegel guy who came today from Jalalabad after organizing his own security (four gunmen in a separate car). He says that the road through the Sarobi Gorge was lined with gunmen who looked crazy, laughing like they were doped up, with long wild hair and very dark skins. He said that they drove past three groups of such fellows who tried to stop them and that they very nearly got caught by the third. He made it, but his security was arranged

through the mayor of Jalalabad. Doing something improvised from here looks dicey.

Basically, this puts us back to square one in terms of any forward movement from Kabul. There are no more UN flights to Islamabad—though, thankfully, the cost has gone down from 2,500 to 600 bucks—until the 19th. I will check on the wait list anyway, even though it means, if one wants to go to Tora Bora, going through Islamabad, then Peshawar, and getting gunmen to go back into Afghanistan and down the Khyber Pass to Jalalabad. A drag, but at least do-able.

From: Jon Lee 12/16/2001
Thomas and I checked our available funds and realized that we have much less than we had thought. A total of 1,900 bucks between us. Just enough, basically, to pay for a convoy that turns out to be leaving tomorrow after all. We have left a 200-dollar deposit. So we have nothing to pay translators, or for vehicles once we are in Jalalabad, or for food or anything. We just paid one translator and might have to borrow some back, we were thinking. A photographer friend of Thomas's may have some money, maybe as much as a thousand, to lend us so that we can get to Pakistan, but we are seriously scraping the bottom of the barrel. Sorry for the last-minute hassle. But that is the situation.

From: Jon Lee 12/17/2001
We are in Jalalabad. Lots of tension but no problems. Still poor, though. I guess we should just stick with the plan of having money wired to Islamabad asap. We will borrow some money here and then get ourselves across the border into Pakistan as best we can.

Holy and Other Warriors

The road from Kabul to Jalalabad follows the Kabul River east for about eighty miles. Fifty miles outside of Kabul, it begins winding through the Sarobi Gorge, where, in January 1842, sixteen thousand British and Indian soldiers and their families were massacred by Afghan tribesmen. The gorge is a dismal, Styxian place, all gray scree and brown dust. The road through it was paved once, but now it is just a narrow dirt-and-rock passageway cut into a mountainside. A mess of giant tumbled boulders and landslides, it falls away on one side to the gray-green river torrent below.

The Sarobi Gorge is one of the most dangerous places in Afghanistan. Bandits and gunmen lie in wait to ambush hapless travellers, whom they rob and sometimes kill. In November, after the fall of Kabul, four journalists who were travelling from Jalalabad were murdered there. In early December, a bus from Jalalabad was said to have been stopped by renegade Taliban who cut off the noses and ears of the male passengers who weren't wearing beards. I wasn't particularly keen to drive through the gorge, a trip that takes six or seven hours, but I wanted to get to

Kandahar, three hundred miles southwest of Kabul, and the direct route was more or less suicidal for Westerners. The Taliban cleared out of Kandahar on December 7, and the next day in Kabul I met a young man who said his name was Nasruddin and that he had just come from Kandahar in a taxi. Nasruddin had seen truckloads of heavily armed Arab Al Qaeda fighters heading in the direction of Khost, near the Pakistan border. The taxi had been stopped several times by Pashtun gunmen dressed in black. Nasruddin, who is a Tajik, assumed that they were Taliban, and he was terrified. He agreed that the only way for me to get to Kandahar was to go to Jalalabad, then cross the border into Pakistan, and reenter Afghanistan farther south, from Quetta, which is linked to Kandahar by a well-travelled road.

The Taliban had vanished from Afghanistan's cities by then, but in much of the countryside, vague new front lines had emerged where the anti-Taliban forces had halted their forward advances. The areas beyond these front lines were no-man's-lands controlled by militias still loyal to the Taliban and by gangs of common bandits, and sometimes by both. This provided an opportunity for enterprising security services, like the one run by Jack, a stocky American in his mid-forties who assembled the convoy to Jalalabad that I joined. Jack—which is not his real name—put together a party of seven journalists who were accompanied by seventeen Afghan fighters from three militias: two from Kabul and one from Sarobi. We each paid him eight hundred dollars. Jack had a mustache and short hair and always wore dark sunglasses and military clothing. A revolver was strapped to his leg in a special holster and he carried an assault rifle. He described himself as a former Green Beret who was working with the new Afghan government as a civilian adviser. Jack wouldn't say whether or not he had any official links to the U.S. armed forces, but he hinted that he enjoyed a cooperative relationship of sorts with the army's counterterrorism task force. He had, he said, been in Afghanistan since September, moving around with the Northern Alliance as they seized territory from the Taliban. Participating in an armed convoy to Jalalabad, he told me, was good training for the Afghans. He hoped to recruit the best of them to become part of an elite Afghan army security corps. "You know," he said, "I'm half hoping we run into some of the bad guys along the way, and that they try to fuck with us, because I'd love nothing better than to let these guys loose on 'em, and kill 'em all."

We saw a few gunmen lurking along the road as we drove through the gorge, their faces shrouded with brown *patou* blankets, and there were others on a crude hilltop bivouac, but none of them interfered with us. They behaved like wild dogs circling a passing herd, hanging back but ready to strike if the opportunity arose. In the end, our convoy made it through to Jalalabad unscathed except for frayed nerves and two flat tires.

JALALABAD IS A BUSTLING, prosperous city of farmers, merchants, and smugglers situated in a fertile river valley two hours by car from the Khyber Pass and the Pakistan border. Snowcapped mountains, including the Tora Bora range to the southeast, surround the valley. Jalalabad is an overwhelmingly Pashtun city, heavily influenced by its proximity to Pakistan, and is distinctly different in style and atmosphere from the provincial Tajik and Uzbek cities of northern Afghanistan, or, for that matter, from the relatively cosmopolitan capital of Kabul, where Tajiks, Uzbeks, and Hazaras, as well as Pashtuns, live in close proximity to one another. Jalalabad's streets are noisy with motorized rickshaws (abundant in Pakistan, scarce in Kabul) and garishly decorated trucks. The signboards of the shop fronts are louder, the bazaar smells spicier. The people have darker skins, wear different clothes, and seem more self-possessed and clannish. Jalalabad's Pashtuns gather around to stare at Westerners—as people do everywhere in Afghanistan—but instead of calling out greetings, they stand quietly, commenting softly among themselves.

Posters of Ahmed Shah Massoud are ubiquitous in northern Afghanistan and in Kabul, but they weren't much in evidence in Jalalabad. Instead of Massoud's image, photographs of a local Pashtun hero, Abdul Haq, hung on electrical poles and on the walls of public buildings. Haq was a mujahideen commander in the anti-Soviet jihad and then became a businessman in Dubai. In October, he returned covertly to Afghanistan with the support of the CIA and began recruiting an anti-Taliban fighting force in his old stomping grounds near Jalalabad, but the Taliban soon captured him and hung him from a chestnut tree just outside of Kabul. The particularly high public esteem held for him may perhaps be explained by the fact that one of his brothers, Haji Abdul Qadir, is the current governor of Nangarhar Province, of which Jalalabad is the capital. Until 1996, when the Taliban seized Jalalabad and he fled into exile in Pakistan, Haji Abdul Qadir was Nangarhar's strongman and head of the so-called Eastern *shura,* a cooperative council of regional mujahideen factions. A wealthy man, he has long been accused of being a major player in the province's flourishing opium trade. Nangarhar is one of Afghanistan's main opium-growing provinces, and it is strategically located next to the heroin refineries that operate just across the border inside Pakistan's freebooting Northwest Frontier Province. The Taliban cracked down on opium cultivation in the summer of 2000, and production was cut drastically.

I had been in Jalalabad during the spring and early summer of 1989, when opium was growing everywhere— entire fields of it, and rectangular patches tucked in among rows of wheat. Jalalabad was then under siege. The Soviets had withdrawn their troops from Afghanistan, but they continued to support the regime of Muhammad Najibullah in Kabul with military aid and advisers, and Soviet pilots still flew bombing missions over Afghanistan. Several mujahideen factions—backed by the United States, Saudi Arabia, and Pakistan—were attempting to gain control of Jalalabad and planned to proclaim themselves the legitimate Afghan government. I was driven through the Khyber Pass by a plainclothes Pakistani agent from Inter-Services Intelligence. He was assisting the mujahideen, and a few days earlier some of them had captured eighty-odd government soldiers and executed them—not a tactic designed to encourage surrender. The front lines nearest the enemy positions—around the Jalalabad airport at the eastern edge of the city—were exposed to enemy fire and manned for the most part by untrained fourteen- and fifteen-year-old boys who had been recruited only weeks earlier from madrasahs in Pakistan's Afghan refugee camps, and they were dying in droves. Occasionally, big white Scud missiles—fired all the way from Kabul—flew in and exploded. Shells, mortars, bullets, bombs, and rockets were landing all over the place, here and there setting the harvest-ready fields of opium and wheat ablaze, sending up great crackling orange curtains of flame and clouds of black smoke.

A group of Arabs were fighting alongside the mujahideen. They had their own camp next to the road that led to the airport. I had not yet heard of Osama bin Laden, but he was apparently there that summer, and those fighters were his men—volunteers for the Islamic crusade against the atheistic regime in Kabul from countries like Egypt, Saudi Arabia, Palestine, Yemen, and Algeria. I drove past a group of them one day when I visited a frontline mujahideen position in an old mud-walled fortress that overlooked Jalalabad's airstrip from a small hill. They were dug into trenches and behind sandbags by the road, weapons pointed, and stared with open hostility as we passed. A couple of hours later, when I was in the fortress, the man we had left with our vehicle came urgently to fetch us: some Arabs had asked if there were any Western *kafirs* in our party. He had told them no, and they had left, but he didn't think they believed him. It was a hunting party, he explained, and we should leave the area immediately because they were likely to come back. We drove past the Arab encampment again. The fighters bristled and glared, but they didn't open fire, probably because I was with a mujahideen escort. The next day, just up the road, an Australian friend was nearly killed by some Arabs who were annoyed that he was witnessing the burial of mujahideen martyrs. Later, I heard stories of other journalists who had encountered the Arabs and had gotten into trouble.

Osama bin Laden and his men, of course, flourished during the Taliban's tenure, only to retreat to their old haunts in the mountains near Jalalabad when the Taliban collapsed. They holed up in caves and bunkers in the Tora Bora mountain range and for more than two weeks fought off several ground offensives by local Afghan mujahideen. They were bombed by U.S. warplanes and hunted down by

American, Australian, Canadian, and British commandos. Then, suddenly, the Al Qaeda men had stopped fighting back, and vanished, presumably fleeing through the high mountains into Pakistan. The American bombing campaign was suspended, and, together with their mujahideen allies, U.S. Special Forces soldiers began a ground search in Tora Bora's snowy ridges for enemy survivors.

OSAMA BIN LADEN had several wives and several houses that, for security reasons, among others, he moved in and out of. One of the houses is in the village of Naji Mujahid, on a desert plain just south of Jalalabad. The house has high mud walls and metal gates. It and a gaggle of similar compounds form a dusty, trash-strewn pit stop strategically located on the jeep track leading to the Tora Bora foothills. Bin Laden's compound is nondescript, a haphazard welter of mud patios and small square houses with spartan rooms and alleyways leading to other cubicles. There were no flower beds, no decorations, and no furniture by the time I arrived. All that had been looted by the local mujahideen. Bin Laden had evidently had plenty of time to gather up his more valuable possessions before he left, and also to burn things he didn't want left lying around. In several places there were blackened swatches of ground and heaps of charred paper.

There were also some unburned papers, and I picked up a page from an English-language Turkish defense magazine with the specifications for an electronic siren and public address system sold by Military Electronics Industries, Inc., of Turkey; an advertisement from the Swedish arms company FFV Ordnance for a tank-busting rocket

A mujahideen in the Tora Bora hills, near Osama bin Laden's house

warhead; an operator's manual for a portable radio transceiver made by Kachina Communications, Inc.; a tax-free shopping receipt for several digital multimeters that cost one hundred and seventy-three deutsche marks, purchased from Conrad Electronic in Munich on May 6, 2000. I also found an article from the November 1989 edition of *Modern Electronics,* entitled: "More on How to Detect Ultraviolet, Visible Light and Infrared," the second of two articles on the subject of radiation.

While I was poking around the compound, accompanied by Jack and a platoon of mujahideen, a sharp-faced young Afghan man and several children wandered in to watch. The man, whose name was Redwarullah, said that he was a neighbor, and he confirmed that until a few weeks earlier the village had been the home of a community of Arab families including that of Osama bin Laden. I asked Redwarullah if he thought bin Laden had masterminded the attacks on the World Trade Center in New York. He said that he didn't think so. "People here thought he was a very nice Muslim," he said. My mujahideen escorts interrupted our chat and led me out of Osama bin Laden's house. They explained that the inhabitants of Naji Mujahid were Al Qaeda supporters, and that it was best not to stay there too long. The next day, we drove up the jeep track beyond the village into a dramatic panorama of ravines and steep, rocky hills covered with scrub oaks and fir trees. Trails led through the diminishing tree line toward the jagged, snow-covered peaks of Tora Bora. It was there that bin Laden's trail had gone cold.

The Afghan mujahideen militias who had been enlisted by the United States to launch the ground attacks at Tora Bora drove their pickups and Russian tanks purposefully around the flanks of the mountains, but there was no action taking place. The Western journalists who had come to witness the much-hyped last stand of Al Qaeda were beginning to pull out of the area. Geraldo Rivera had moved on. The tent city erected for the press on a wind-blown lower ridge of the mountain was littered with satellite dishes, plastic bottles, cans, and wrappers of imported foodstuffs. It looked like a climbers' base camp in the Himalayas, but it was shrinking, a process that had been hastened by a number of assaults and robberies perpetrated by the increasingly unruly mujahideen.

Up in the mountains, some Afghan fighters and a handful of reporters wandered cautiously around the site of a bomb-blasted Al Qaeda training camp. There were still Al Qaeda men in the vicinity, by all accounts. Some had attacked this very spot in broad daylight a couple of days earlier, sending mujahideen and journalists scattering for cover. Most of the trees that were still standing had been literally peeled, their branches shorn of twigs and bark by explosions, and what had been caves and underground bunkers was now an uncertain welter of mounds and holes. There was also the confused refuse left behind by human beings: pieces of ripped camouflage clothing, sleeping bags, hundreds of tin ammunition boxes with Chinese lettering, the yellow tags of unexploded cluster bomblets, and bits of paper. Here and there lay sections—huge ones—of American bomb casings. In the distance I could see an Afghan man chopping up the ravaged trees with an ax, preparing to cart the kindling away. The next day, a scavenger was blown in half by a partially buried bomblet.

I picked up a bull's-eye that had been used for target shooting; some handwritten notes about ammunition supplies; an instruction sheet for Negram, a medicine for urinary and intestinal infections; and an English-language

phrasebook for Arabic speakers. The phrasebook was illustrated with cartoonlike scenes peopled with men wearing suits and homburgs. Their faces had been inked out.
Looking through the book, I wondered about the utility of
some of phrases bin Laden's warriors had learned: "It is
nice to listen to good music on the radio"; "Plenty of brush-
ing improves your hair"; "I am trying to keep the room
clean, but he keeps putting things on the piano"; "Please
don't speak to my dog unkindly." It was hard to imagine
an Al Qaeda volunteer living up in this bleak mountain-
scape, praying devoutly five times daily, medicating himself against stomach ailments while learning how to shoot
properly, and, in his free moments, boning up on his English so that, presumably, he would at some future date
be able to negotiate his way into a Western country like
England or the United States to carry out an atrocious
mission in which he would most likely die.

On the way down the mountain, Jack, who was armed
and wearing full combat regalia, clambered onto one of the
mujahideen tanks with a tin of white paint and a brush. He
wrote "N.Y.P.D." on the tank's green steel carapace. The
mujahideen smiled obligingly and asked to borrow his
paint. In lacy Farsi script they added the words "Dear
Massoud, we will follow your way."

THE HOTEL SPINGHAR IN JALALABAD is a faded late-Deco place
surrounded by a grove of orange trees. The image of a
Kalashnikov with a red X over it, like a no-smoking sign,
has been pasted onto the wall outside the front door. A
portrait of a regional warlord, Hazrat Ali, a wiry man with
a graying beard, hangs inside, next to the reception desk.
Hazrat Ali is said to be the Spinghar's owner, though how

he acquired the hotel is something of a mystery. He was the leader of a band of anti-Taliban guerrillas in the hills outside Jalalabad, and when the Taliban and their Al Qaeda allies fled town in the middle of November he led his fighters into the city. In the subsequent division of political spoils, Hazrat Ali, who is a member of the Northern Alliance, became the security chief for the Eastern *shura,* which controls Nangarhar Province in loose cooperation with the Karzai regime in Kabul. Hazrat Ali was the favorite local proxy fighter of the U.S. Special Forces advisers in the fighting at Tora Bora.

I met Commander Ali the day he gave an impromptu press conference in a banquet room of the hotel. He wore a waxed hunting jacket with a gray fleece lining and was surrounded by a retinue of gunmen. He spoke with bluff bravado, declaring that Al Qaeda was "no longer a problem," then seemed to hedge, admitting that terrorists might be able to infiltrate the ranks of his own fighting force. "This is a danger we must be on the alert for." Hazrat Ali may well have been preempting the rumors that were already beginning to circulate that some of his men had assisted the escape of hundreds of Al Qaeda terrorists from Tora Bora into Pakistan. "God only knows where Osama bin Laden is now," he said, lamely.

Hazrat Ali ended the press conference with what sounded like a backhanded warning to his new sponsors. "If the U.S. tries to take over the suppression of all the Al Qaeda activities in Afghanistan by itself, in my view this will bring it problems similar to the ones experienced by the Soviets in Afghanistan. But if the United States supports the popular resistance forces who have been fighting terrorism in Afghanistan for many years, then I am sure the people will be happy with that."

That night I met Hazrat Ali's eldest son, Samiullah, a handsome and self-possessed twenty-two-year-old who is a military commander in his own right, with two hundred fighters and a crew of bodyguards. "Osama and his troops were so well entrenched that it was not easy rooting them out," he said. "We were fighting them on the ground, but their deep caves made it difficult. The American air support helped a lot." Samiullah insisted that American soldiers had not done the real fighting for the caves. "The U.S. Special Forces are only here as target spotters, not fighters," he said, "and even so they have caused many casualties from their bombs among the mujahideen—even more than those caused by Al Qaeda." Like his father, Samiullah was unenthusiastic about more overt American involvement on the ground. "My forces are sensitive about the presence of foreigners," he said. "If big numbers of Americans come here, I think the people will react against them."

Hazrat Ali gave Jack and me permission to visit some Al Qaeda prisoners in the Jalalabad jail. The mujahideen guarding the door at the jail didn't want to let us in but finally said we could stay for fifteen minutes. The day before, news had reached Jalalabad that a group of Al Qaeda fighters who had been caught on the other side of the border with Pakistan had overpowered the guards on a bus that was transporting them to Peshawar. They had seized their guns, killed several of them, and caused the bus to crash. A number of these Al Qaeda fighters had escaped and were still at large.

It was a brilliant winter day. Birds sang in the trees. We entered an unkempt garden planted with ratty rosebushes and shaded by large mulberry trees with orange leaves. At the end of the garden, armed sentries stood in

front of a fortresslike brick building with big gray gates and
crenellated parapets. Several mujahideen officials came up
to us and laid out ground rules for our visit. They explained
that the prisoners were dangerous. "They have already
tried to take away our guns," one official said. They would
select a couple of prisoners to speak to us, and bring them
out in handcuffs and ankle chains.

While we waited for the prisoners to appear, a man approached me and asked me, slyly, if I wanted to see something. He showed me a passport. It belonged to one of the
terrorists, he said, and he wished to sell it. It was a brand-
new Algerian passport, issued in 2001, with a picture of a
neat young man of Arab appearance named Salim Yahiaqui
who had been born in 1979. It described his profession as
"photographer." The man snatched it back after I had noted
down these details. He stuffed it into his jacket pocket and
moved away. A few minutes later the doors of the prison
opened, and a dozen or so men came out. We were told to
walk toward them, and our two groups met on the footpath
of the garden and formed a large circle. Someone pointed
out the two prisoners for me. One was a short, stocky man
with a black beard and pitted olive skin. He wore a dirty
black anorak, a gray *shalwar kameez,* camouflage fatigue
trousers, and new black leather boots. A stocking cap partially covered his thick black hair, which was uncombed and
dirty. He stared intently at us. The other prisoner was taller
and thinner and older looking, with a vague expression. Neither man was handcuffed or wore ankle chains, which I
found alarming, since they were only a few feet away from
us and right next to mujahideen who were armed but who
seemed less than attentive about their duties as guards. The
younger prisoner was watchful and self-confident; he had a
half smile that was not quite a sneer, but almost.

One of the Afghans began speaking to the prisoners in Arabic, explaining who we were, and telling them that we wanted to hear their stories. The younger man said his name was Faiz Muhammad Ahmed, that he was twenty-six years old, and was from Kuwait. He spoke in Arabic, but it soon became evident that he understood English as well, because he occasionally corrected the interpreter. "The international community is mistaken about Arabs in Afghanistan," he said. "Not all are here for Osama bin Laden." He was a businessman. "I have a lot of money, and I came to Afghanistan to help Muslims. I came to dig wells." When Jalalabad fell he had met some Arabs. "These Arabs, who I didn't know, said I should go to the mountains with them, and so I did and that's when I was caught." The interpreter laughed as he translated this, and put his hand on the Kuwaiti's shoulder in a matey kind of way. Faiz Muhammad Ahmed stared at us with his half smile.

"This is hardly credible," I said.

"But it is a big mistake to say all Arabs in Afghanistan are with Osama bin Laden and are terrorists," Faiz Muhammad Ahmed replied. "It would be as if we said, 'All Westerners in Afghanistan are CIA.' " He glanced toward Jack, and added, "Maybe you are."

If he was a businessman, as he claimed, I asked, why was he dressed as he was? "My normal clothes were blown up by the American bombing," he explained. What was his opinion of Osama bin Laden and Al Qaeda? "I personally do not agree with Osama bin Laden's policy; it is against the Koran," he said. "But I also think that the U.S. is at fault for attacking Muslims. I am an eyewitness of American bombing against civilians in Afghanistan." Then he said that he would like to send a message though us.

Jack interrupted, angrily: "No! You sent a message to us on September eleventh!" I argued with Jack about letting the man speak, and he relented. Given his opportunity, Faiz Muhammad Ahmed made a statement: "I want to say that I am from Kuwait and that I have been to the United States. My background should be checked out and I should be sent to Kuwait for trial."

The second prisoner said that his name was Nassir Abdel Latif. He was from Casablanca, Morocco, and was thirty-six years old. He wore a camouflage jacket and U.S. Special Forces combat boots and a gray *pakul* cap. He spoke in a neutral and matter-of-fact tone of voice. "I came to Afghanistan because of Afghanistan's strict Islamic rule and because it was full of Islamic scholars," he said. He had come to live, not fight, in Afghanistan, he stressed, but he happened to be in Kabul when it fell, and then he escaped to Jalalabad, and when it also fell he had to flee to the mountains.

We asked if he had been fighting when he was caught. "Yes," he said. "By then I was carrying a gun. I was a military man." But, he added, unconvincingly, he didn't know the identity of the group he was with in the mountains. "We not only condemn Osama bin Laden," he said, "but Israel too. You people should remember that there are some actions which made Osama bin Laden carry out *his* action."

Faiz Muhammad Ahmed interrupted. "The Al Qaeda didn't keep their people with us," he said. "Al Qaeda takes its people to a big secret place in the mountains. There are a lot of secret things in Al Qaeda."

The guards were listening, but they didn't seem to notice that Faiz Muhammad Ahmed had inched forward.

He moved forward slightly all the time we were talking, and I kept stepping back from him. The whole circle of men moved perhaps two feet during our forty-minute encounter.

I asked Nassir Abdel Latif if he was a member of Al Qaeda. "I was in military training camps," he said. "First in Casablanca, and then in Kabul. Then I was a businessman, and when I came to Kabul I was living in a training camp, but not actually training." When I asked him what kind of business he was involved in, he replied, vaguely, that he had been doing business between Libya and Sudan, and had then gone to Yemen and from there to Pakistan, and finally had arrived in Afghanistan. Nassir Abdel Latif then acknowledged that he had received military training in Kabul after all, and told us that the place he had been living was called the Libyan Jihadi Military Training Camp. He *had* been a businessman once, he said, but in the end had wanted to be a fighter.

Jack asked to see the palms of the men's hands and concluded that they both were fighters. "This is from holding a Kalashnikov," he said, pointing to Faiz Muhammad Ahmed's calluses.

I asked if either of them had seen Osama bin Laden. Faiz Muhammad Ahmed said no, but Nassir Abdel Latif said that he had: "He was in Tora Bora for a long time and he was receiving a lot of visitors. Osama bin Laden told us: 'Believe in us, believe in Allah, believe in me, in this jihad, we will win in the end.'" Nassir Abdel Latif stared at me directly with his pale brown eyes. "We did not come here to fight Afghans, we came here to fight Americans, and we will keep fighting until we destroy them totally."

That seemed to make Jack happy, and Faiz Muhammad Ahmed tried to qualify things. "Most of us who were on Tora

Bora wanted to fight Americans," he said, "but not all Americans. Just those who are fighting Muslims." I asked him if Osama bin Laden was still alive. "God only knows," he said. And then our meeting was at an end. Jack raised his hand and wagged a finger at them. "America will come and get you," he said. They didn't reply.

JACK'S CORPS OF AFGHAN BODYGUARDS was an unruly group. They squabbled among themselves or with Jack over food and money, and once some of them threatened to kill Jack's irritating young interpreter for trying to order them around. Jack told the boy to keep his mouth shut and to stick to translating what he said. But problems cropped up every day, and after some altercation with the fighters Jack turned to me and remarked, "Compared with the Afghans, the Haitians were fuckin' easy. You just told 'em, 'Do this, motherfucker!' And they said 'OK!' But not these guys." He shook his head.

Jack was extremely critical of the way the U.S. military had handled things at Tora Bora. They had allowed undisciplined, untrained, and ill-equipped Afghans to carry out the bulk of the fighting while they remained in the background. "If we don't fucking send in some American advisers here quick we're gonna be right back to where we were five years from now," he said. "We failed the Afghans after the Russians left. We didn't do any demobilization and normalization. There's tens of thousands of soldiers and commanders with guns in this country! What're you gonna do with 'em? Instead of sending in five thousand British peacekeepers, we should send in a hundred instructors to teach them how to do it themselves. All these guys need is professional training. The less training an army has, the more dangerous it is."

Jack said that he was was born in upstate New York and that he lived now in Fayetteville, North Carolina. He was forty-six and had joined the Green Berets in 1974, when he was nineteen. "I spent twenty-five years in Special Operations in one form or another," he said. "Except for a brief period in which I was trying to be cop." Was he still active-duty, or was he retired? "I have no official relationship to the U.S. government," he said, as if by rote. We played cat and mouse on this question, but Jack told me some of the places he had been as a U.S. military adviser. "I trained the U.S. Marine security mission in Haiti in 1980," he said. He had spent time in El Salvador, as well. "I was in Vilnius, Lithuania, during the coup in January ninety-one; also at the Moscow coup in August ninety-one. I was just there as assistance to pro-U.S. forces—with the Alpha group teams in Moscow. They were on the good guys' side, the anti-Communists." He had been involved in the Gulf War, as well. A couple of years ago, he'd resigned his Special Forces commission. "I was getting too old to carry a rucksack, and I had broken my back and my neck."

So why was he in Afghanistan? "I just said I was goin' one way or another, to some people in DOD"—the Department of Defense—he replied. His first mission was to provide ground assistance to the air drops of U.S. humanitarian aid rations. He had also conducted an investigation into the rumors circulating among Afghans that the rations were poisoned.

"I found out who did it," Jack said, "and it was not Al Qaeda or the Taliban. And there wasn't any poison. The people were eating the desiccant"—the preservative drying agent—"that comes in little packets in each ration pack.

It says, 'Do Not Eat' in English, French, Spanish, and Chinese. But not in Farsi or Pashto. They thought it was spices! So there were some severe injuries and several presumed deaths. One guy who died ate the Handi Wipes, the desiccant—everything. These people, I mean, they don't even have napkins, how do they know what a Handi Wipe is? I gather he thought it smelled good, so he ate it." Other people had become ill, Jack found, because many of the ration packs had exploded on impact, and the food inside had been exposed and become contaminated. Jack said that he wrote a report that was sent to DOD, and about a week later the problems were sorted out.

"When that was over," Jack said, "I went back to doing what I normally do, which is to advise foreign armies."

From: Jon Lee 12/24/2001
Well, yes, Merry Christmas. Certainly doesn't feel like one here in about-to-be-nuked-inshallah Pakistan. I figure that you are still out shopping, so will have dinner and call you later. Have been writing a bit, but don't have anything to send you yet. The days are chopped up ad nauseam with waits for visa extensions and money. (Got both, but it took all day today.) We are going to Quetta tomorrow. Good hotel there, the Serena. Qias is already there and has met a smuggler/fixer whose name I had. He says he seems OK. So we'll meet him tomorrow and maybe go in on Thursday. More later.

From: Jon Lee 12/25/2001
Remember to drink something for me, since I am a very parched soul at this point. We are in Quetta. Nice place. I stayed here thirteen years ago, precisely. The Serena is a kind of Pakistani-Santa-Fe-style hotel. We've met our "smuggler," who has a Ph.D. in Political Science and teaches English. Seems very good. I am going to stay in and write tomorrow and catch up, and he and Thomas are going out to the border to arrange things with his contacts so that there will be no contretemps on Friday, when we leave. It's a

whole-day affair, so Saturday will be our first working day. All best. Happy Holidays.

From: Jon Lee 12/27/2001
Hi. Just to say that we've arrived in Kandahar without incident. Got through all the checkpoints in our disguises. Buses passed us covered with Osama bin Laden posters, and there were lots of Talib-looking guys everywhere. Weird. We are now in what is practically the only hotel in this rather small, beat-up city.

Mullah Omar's Favorite Songs

I n the winter of 1988–89, I spent a month in a mujahideen camp in the Argandhab Valley, a few miles north of Kandahar. The Soviets had begun to withdraw their troops from Afghanistan, but MiG warplanes were still carrying out daily bombing and strafing runs, and in the slummy southern suburbs of Kandahar there was a front line where both sides were dug in. The commander of the camp, Mullah Naquibullah, known as Naquib, was a tall, beefy fellow, the chief of Kandahar's second-largest tribe, the Alokozai. He had installed about thirty of his fighters on the outskirts of his home village of Charqulba. The village itself was mostly destroyed and abandoned; nearly all the inhabitants had fled to refugee camps in Pakistan. The only civilians in the area were a few Kutchi nomad families who wandered around with their camels and herds of goats. The desert was pocked from years of Soviet bombardment, and unexploded rockets stuck out of the earth at odd angles here and there, like children's arrows. Naquib's camp consisted of half a dozen flat-roofed mud huts and a prayer ground in the midst of vineyards. The day before I arrived, a bomb had landed nearby, leaving a huge crater in which a beautiful black stallion lay dead, its hooves in the air.

The war, such as it was, was fairly abstract by then. You could see bombs exploding in the distance most days, but there was no real threat of ground attacks from the besieged government garrison, and Mullah Naquib pretty much had the run of the Argandhab Valley. His mujahideen prayed diligently five times a day, and, given their devotion and their abstinent way of life, I began to think of them as warrior monks.

One day Naquib sent me off to observe a court session led by two elderly Islamic scholars who were charged with imposing Sharia, religious law, in the region. I was driven at breakneck speed along a bombed-out road by a young man who played tapes of wailing Kandahari love songs at high volume on the cassette deck of a Toyota pickup truck. The court was set up out-of-doors, in the shade of a raisin-storage silo. The judges leaned on pillows propped up against the silo walls and told me how they followed the Koran in reaching verdicts about territorial rights, adultery, theft, and so forth. After some bickering over numbers, they agreed that they had put eighteen murderers to death. Their discourse on justice went on for some time, and then the younger of the two produced a piece of paper and announced that a new edict was being sent to all the mujahideen commanders in the region. Crime had increased, and this was due, they believed, to the playing of recorded music, which was banned from now on.

The ban obviously came as a shock to the mujahideen who had accompanied me. They looked embarrassed but didn't say much, and we left as soon as the court broke for lunch. Driving back to Naquib's camp, the young driver pointedly inserted a tape into the cassette deck and turned the volume up even louder than it had been before. I learned later that Naquib told his men that he was not going to make a big issue of the new edict. He said that they could continue to play music, but only when they were in camp, and that they should keep it low. Meanwhile, he told the judges that he would comply with their order. Naquib's pragmatic way of dealing with the situation seemed to me admirable.

I thought of that rustic court recently when I visited Mullah Naquib in Kandahar, where he has been living on and off since 1992, when the Communist-backed Afghan regime was finally defeated. Naquib is a controversial figure in Kandahar because of his relationship with the Taliban. When Burhanuddin Rabbani was president of Afghanistan, Naquib was made the supreme military commander of Kandahar, but in 1994 he turned the city over to the Taliban. Many people believe that he was also involved in the recent, unexplained disappearance of the Taliban from Kandahar, and they blame him especially for the escape of Mullah Omar.

Naquib didn't remember me at first, but when he did he seemed pleased, and he began introducing me as a friend from the old days of the jihad against the Soviets. Naquib has aged badly; although he is only forty-seven, he looks much older. He wears glasses now, and his long black beard is streaked with gray. He has a bad cough. We reminisced for a while, and he offered to take me back to the Argandhab Valley to revisit the mujahideen camp where we had met more than a decade earlier. The next day, followed by a dozen or so bodyguards, he led me to the carport in his living compound, where two late-model SUVs were parked. We got into a pearl-colored VX Limited Edition Toyota Land Cruiser, and several small boys, the youngest of Naquib's eleven children, climbed into the back. The Toyota had a sunroof and a luxurious tan leather interior and a CD player with an LCD display. It was a fine car, I said to Naquib. He chuckled. "It was Mullah Omar's," he said. "I have ten of his cars."

We took off, and I asked Naquib how he had come to own Mullah Omar's cars. "They were just parked, so I took them," he replied, somewhat glibly. We came to a gate on the security perimeter of Mullah Omar's property, which turned out to be more or less next door. The sentries at the gate saluted Naquib. Mullah Omar apparently owned a hundred acres or so on the edge of town, with about ten acres given over to a compound of living quarters and guest houses that were surrounded by a maze of walls. We drove down a dirt road that runs through Omar's property, and soon came to the paved road to the Argandhab Valley, a rural fastness where dusty tracks lead off in all directions into the desert and the mountain ranges beyond. Omar's house was well placed for a getaway.

I asked Naquib if he had met Mullah Omar. "Lots of times," he said. He described him as "a very quiet man who never spoke to people."

As we drove through a pass between the mountains just behind Omar's land, Naquib turned on the CD player, and the Toyota was filled with Afghan music. I asked if the CD was his or had come with the car.

"It was here when I got it," Naquib said, opening the CD storage container on the armrest between the front seats. We looked for secular music among the discs of keening prayers, and fiddled with the sound system for a while.

"Are you telling me," I said, when we had made a selection, "that this stuff belonged to the man who put people in prison for listening to music?" Naquib shrugged. "It seems so." The song that was playing, he said, was a popular Afghan tune that vilified General Rashid Dostum, the Uzbek warlord from Mazar-i-Sharif. Its chief refrain was "O murderer of the Afghan people."

"What is life without music?" Mullah Naquib said.

MANY VESTIGES OF THE TALIBAN ERA remain untouched in the beat-up, dusty center of Kandahar, where the ruins of buildings that collapsed during the recent American bombing campaign lie among the ruins of older battles. Vendors with carts sell "Super Osama bin Laden Kulfa Balls"—coconut candy manufactured in Pakistan and packaged in pink-and-purple boxes covered with images of bin Laden surrounded by tanks, cruise missiles, and jet fighters. The chaotic streets are full of men who look like Taliban, with white or black turbans and big, bushy beards. They roar around in Toyota pickups adorned with flags with green, black, and red stripes—the old royalist flag of Afghanistan, which has been revived by the followers of Hamid Karzai, the interim prime minister—and there is no way, really, to know their past affiliations. In Kandahar, as in most other parts of Afghanistan, the Taliban didn't surrender so much as melt away. The leaders vanished, but most rank-and-file members simply returned to their homes. Karzai promised not to persecute former Taliban who stopped fighting, and he has kept his word. Kandahar is officially Taliban-free, but it has an unreconciled atmosphere. The past has not quite been overcome, and the future is unresolved.

The mausoleum that adjoins the Ahmed Shah mosque, which is across the street from the governor's palace, has a special subterranean chamber that *kafirs* cannot enter. It houses the cloak that is believed to have belonged to the Prophet Muhammad. On April 4, 1996, when Mullah Omar was declared the Keeper of the Faithful, he took the cloak out of the chamber and, in a dramatic display of hubris, donned it before a crowd of spectators. It was one of the few times that Omar appeared in public. I met only one person in Kandahar, besides Mullah Naquib, who had ever seen him. This was a young man named Popal, who worked at the governor's palace. Popal kept me company one evening as I waited for an interview with Gul Agha Shirzai, who had been appointed governor of Kandahar in mid-December. Popal brought me tea, and we sat together on the floor of a large office. He apologized for the lack of chairs, and explained that the Taliban had taken virtually everything when they left—even the carpets. The cheap imitation Persian we were sitting on, he said, had been bought in the bazaar. "And those"—he pointed to some computer monitors, keyboards, and printers—"we got from some of the Arabs' houses." He was referring to members of Al Qaeda, several hundred of whom had lived in Kandahar. I noticed that none of the computers had towers. "The Americans who have a base here, just behind the palace," Popal said, "are checking the hard drives for information, and when they are done they will give them to us."

The city was crawling with Americans, mostly marines, who drove around in heavily armed convoys of sand-colored Humvees, their guns pointed and their faces masked by black balaclavas. There were also small groups of weather-beaten Special Forces commandos, who wore Afghan clothes and drove Toyota four-wheel-drive pickups. From a distance, they were hard to distinguish from the many mujahideen fighters in town. They kept to themselves.

Popal had worked at the palace under the Taliban, too. It was hard to find a job in Kandahar. His long-term goal, he said, was to improve his English, so that he could become an English-Pashto translator, and also to learn computer programming. These were both things that had been nearly impossible to do under the Taliban. "The Taliban wanted us to learn Arabic. They let us work with computers, but we could not use CDs or any programs that showed human images." He said that once, a few years back, he had been stopped by the Taliban's religious police, who said that his beard was too short. They had taken him to a building and told him that his head was going to be shaved as punishment. "The building had no running water, but there was a drainage ditch outside, full of sewage, and they made me wet my hair from it and they used a razor to shave my head. It was very dirty water."

Popal said that many Taliban officials had fled to the nearby Pakistani city of Quetta, and a few days earlier several of them, including the Taliban minister of justice, had dispatched representatives to Kandahar to meet with the new governor. "You see, the Pakistani authorities are now bothering them, saying they must leave Pakistan. So they sent their people to meet with Mr. Gul Agha Shirzai and they told him where they had hidden weapons and vehicles in Kandahar. And they asked Mr. Gul Agha Shirzai to ask the Pakistani authorities, on their behalf, to allow them to stay there. He has sent those letters today, I believe." This was a couple of weeks before the Taliban minister of justice and other Taliban officials turned up in Kandahar and were sent home by Gul Agha, much to the dismay of the Americans.

Popal had met Mullah Omar at the governor's palace. "I remember he arrived in a Toyota Corolla that belonged to someone else," Popal said. "A normal car. He came here because the father of one of the officials was ill and he wanted to wish him well. He was very quiet, gentle. He seemed to me like a good man, not like those other Taliban who shaved my head with the drainage water."

THE AUSTERITY OF THE TALIBAN was particularly anomalous in the Pashtun homelands of eastern and southern Afghanistan, of which Kandahar is the principal city. Mosques, for instance, are more architecturally ornate in the Pashtun region than they are in the north. The streets are filled with motorized rickshaws covered with fanciful bronze embossing and shiny decals. Trucks are decorated with painted tin panels and wooden bulwarks like the prows of old-fashioned schooners. Metal gewgaws dangling from their fenders tinkle as the trucks lumber along.

Pashtun men, Kandaharis in particular, are very conscious of their personal appearance. Many of them line their eyes with black kohl and color their toenails, and sometimes their fingernails, with henna. Some also dye their hair. It is quite common to see otherwise sober-seeming older men with long beards that are a flaming, almost punklike orange color. Burly, bearded men who carry weapons also wear *chaplis,* colorful high-heeled sandals. I noticed that to be really chic in Kandahar you wear your *chaplis* a size or so too small, which means that you mince and wobble as you walk.

Afghans from other regions joke about the high incidence of pederasty among Kandahari men. They say that when crows fly over Kandahar they clamp one wing over their bottoms, just in case. One of the first things the Taliban did—a popular move—was to punish mujahideen commanders who were accused of rape or pederasty. Homosexuals who were sentenced to death faced a particularly grisly end. Tanks or bulldozers crushed them and buried them under mud walls. Pederasty was evidently a continuing source of concern to Mullah Omar, who decreed that Taliban commanders couldn't have beardless boys in their ranks.

In downtown Kandahar, directly across from a row of small bakeries and the run-down Noor Jehan hotel, Kandahar's finest, there are several hole-in-the-wall photo shops. After the exodus of the Taliban from the city in early December, the proprietors hung portraits of their clients in the windows, along with photographs of famous people like Bruce Lee, Leonardo DiCaprio, Ahmed Shah Massoud, and King Zahir Shah. There are many portraits of Taliban fighters posing in front of curtains or painted backdrops. They hold guns and bouquets of plastic flowers. Some are alone, others are with a friend. Some sit rigidly side by side and a few have their arms draped over one another, and some even clasp their hands together affectionately.

Said Kamal, the proprietor of the Photo Shah Zada shop, did a brisk business in Taliban portraits. He specializes in retouched photos. Kamal's artful brushwork removes blemishes and adds color. The backdrops of his portraits are vivid greens or blues with halos of red and orange, and clothing has been transformed from the drab to the garish. Many of the Taliban sat for their portraits with heavily kohled eyes, which made them look like silent-movie stars.

Taliban portraits lie under the glass of Said Kamal's front counter and hang on the wall in tin frames. He said that they belong to Taliban who fled the city, and he doesn't expect them to be picked up. I found this confusing, since Mullah Omar had enforced the Koranic prohibition on representations of the human image, but Said Kamal explained

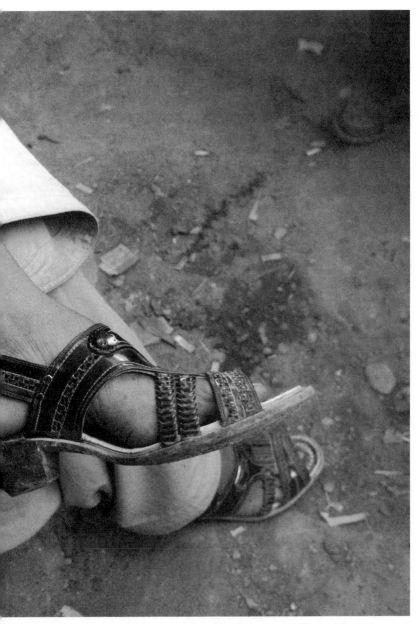

A Kandahari man in chaplis, *high-heeled sandals*

that after the ban on images was announced, and the Taliban forced the photo shops to shut down, they realized that even they needed passport pictures. There was no way around it, if they wanted to travel. So an exception was made to Mullah Omar's edict. Officially, Said Kamal made passport photographs, and he formally complied with the rules, displaying no pictures of human beings in his shop window. But the rules were never fully obeyed by everyone. Said Kamal continued to make portraits of the Taliban, just as he continued to take clandestine wedding pictures at the request of ordinary Kandaharis.

I VISITED MULLAH OMAR'S COMPOUND by myself one day after Mullah Naquib had pointed it out. It had been heavily bombed and strafed and rocketed, and untidy piles of bricks and masonry lay everywhere, but the section in which Mullah Omar lived with his wives and children was mostly still intact, thanks to twelve-foot-thick bombproof roofs. Construction materials for future additions and improvements lay alongside the debris. Mullah Omar had had plans. He wanted to make the desert bloom. Scores of young shade saplings were planted along the driveways, and there were several flower gardens inside the compound. At one of the guest houses, a tanker truck pumped water onto a bed of geraniums. The words "Donated by UNICEF to Kandahar Water Supply Department" were written on the side of the truck. The men holding the hose told me that they had been coming to water Omar's gardens for some time.

A pickup truck came by. Several RPG antitank rockets stood upright on either side of the cab, and an armed American wearing a black turban was sitting in the back.

A U.S. soldier who appeared to be in his late thirties told me that the part of the compound in front of me was off limits but that I could walk around the part where Mullah Omar's living quarters were. "You can't miss it," he said. "It's the place that looks like Motel 6."

In front of Omar's house there is a small concrete mosque with several minarets, domed cupolas, and pillars with huge flowers painted on them. A sculpture of a fallen tree and boulders, painted black and green, serves as a kind of traffic island between the mosque and the house. Two or three faux date palms jut up around the sculpture, which seems to serve also as a fountain, although it was dry on the day I visited. The outer walls of the house are covered with murals depicting lakes and ornamental gardens and more flowers. Omar lived with his favorite wife in a private apartment on one side of the house, painted, for the most part, pink and green. The floor is covered with plastic terrazzo tiles. The bedroom, which is small and dank, has a ceiling fan, a double bed, and two white and faux gilt mini-chandeliers. Several mujahideen were resting on Omar's bed when I poked my head in; they got up quickly and adjusted their turbans. On the other side of the house, I was told, three more wives had lived with their several children. These rooms were much plainer, and there was only one, rather crude flower painted on a wall of the common hallway.

Down the road, at Mullah Naquib's house, one of his bodyguards, a sun-darkened and rough-hewn man in black, showed me Naquib's flower garden in an inner courtyard. There were clumps of carefully tended roses, daffodils, and dahlias, and I complimented him on their beauty. The bodyguard smiled. "This is what we've grown with hardly any water, but you should see it when we have rain."

* * *

THE DAY NAQUIB DROVE ME to the Argandhab Valley to visit the old mujahideen camp, I recognized landmarks such as the tomb of Baba Wali—a holy man whose shrine is on top of a hill that during the jihad was part of Naquib's domain—but there were many more trees than I remembered, and cultivated fields, and more people, too. Naquib said that most of the people who had fled to Pakistan during the war had returned. Now it was drought, not war, that was the problem. We drove along dirt tracks between vineyards, and then walked across fields to where the camp had been. "We've plowed it all under to grow grapes," Naquib said. The only house left standing was the one where he had slept. In the intervening years, he had bought more land. He had inherited only ten jeribs from his father, but now he owned two hundred and fifty, about a hundred and twenty-five acres. He was growing wheat, grapes, almonds, and pomegranates.

Naquib's grandfather, and his father, too, had been the head of the Alokozai tribe, but during Zahir Shah's reign a *malek,* a government administrator, was appointed. Then, after the anti-Soviet jihad began, things reverted to the way they had been. Naquib said that a man named Azizullah Wasfi, who had moved to the United States, is the official tribal elder, but that in his absence Naquib was put in charge.

I asked Naquib to whom the tribal authority would pass when Azizullah Wasfi died. "Well, when the tribe appoints a leader, it chooses someone who can serve them," he said. "I am not so interested in doing this, because of health problems, but I will help if I am asked." Naquib said that his duties were "resolving disputes and grievances." For example, he said, "when Mullah Omar decided to leave Kandahar, he came to me as leader of the Alokozai." Almost as an afterthought, Naquib added, "The tribal chief also can call up the men for war." There were Alokozai all over the place, not only in Argandhab but in the neighboring provinces of Oruzgan, Helmand, and even, he said, as far away as Herat.

For a couple of hours, we walked from one share-cropper's home to another. Invariably, the peasants kissed Naquib's hand deferentially. He inspected irrigation systems and asked questions and gave orders. Then we drove to his house, near the village of Charqulba, and sat on large mats and cushions that his men fetched for us. His bodyguards fanned out vigilantly, and we talked about what had happened to him after I left Afghanistan. Apparently everything had gone well at first. "But then the civil war started, and during the chaos the Taliban appeared. When the Taliban movement started, Hamid Karzai came to see me and told me not to fight against them. And Rabbani also called me and told me not to fight. At the time, we all thought the Talib were fighting for the king"—for the restoration of Zahir Shah to the throne—"and they told me, 'You should surrender the garrison and your guns.' Rabbani wasn't sending money or ammunition to me. How could anyone fight against the Taliban under those conditions?"

After he handed over Kandahar, Naquib said, the Taliban ordered him to go back to Charqulba to live. "I stayed here for a few years, and then I was wounded in an assassination attempt, and went to Islamabad for treatment." Naquib pulled up a sleeve and a trouser leg to show me his scars. He'd been hit by a bullet in his left leg and another in his left elbow, and he pointed to his chest, where, he said, he'd received a rocket fragment. The six men travelling with him had been killed; he was the only survivor. The attackers had been apprehended, he told me. "They claimed that it had been a case of mistaken identity. They said they thought I was a Taliban official." Naquib shrugged, and continued with his story: "I stayed in Islamabad for about two years, and Hamid Karzai and I met with some American officials there. The Americans wanted to know about Al Qaeda, so that they could act against it. We also met with the Italian ambassador. They all told us they would not let Pakistan interfere anymore in our country. And afterward, when I returned home to Kandahar, Hamid Karzai stayed in touch with me."

Naquib lived in Kandahar for about two years after his return from Pakistan, he said. "But then when September eleventh happened, and the Americans started bombing, I came to this house in the village, and I was in touch with Hamid Karzai. He gave me a satellite phone." In early December, Naquib said, when Karzai was chosen as Afghanistan's interim leader, "Mullah Omar and the Taliban agreed to leave, and Karzai agreed that the Taliban would transfer power in Kandahar to me. But by the morning after the night the BBC announced the transfer, the Taliban had all left. Gul Agha entered the city, and Karzai appointed him governor and myself corps commander. I have some health problems, so I refused the job, and gave it to my deputy, Khan Muhammad."

The competition between Mullah Naquib and Gul Agha had been intense, and many people had expected fighting to break out between them in the days after the Taliban left the city, but Naquib insisted that he had no bad feelings toward Gul Agha, and I didn't press him, because he seemed to like his version of events and wasn't about to change it. He was more candid about his health problems, which were "mental." He had been to two hospitals in Germany for treatment. "I was crazy," he said, and laughed, and all the men who were gathered around now, listening to us, laughed, too, evidently at the memory of his behavior. "I was not myself. I would get tense and have headaches. The doctors told me that I had a heavy workload and it had damaged some of my brain cells." Naquib's symptoms had appeared after the Taliban took over Kandahar, but he said that the problems might have been caused by the explosion of a Russian mortar shell near him during the jihad. "A piece of the shell hit me here," he said, pointing to his forehead. "It was just a small piece, but maybe it had something to do with it." He pulled out a strip of capsules. He had been given a prescription for Risperdal, an antipsychotic. "Each pill costs three hundred rupees," he said, or about four and a half dollars.

EARLY ONE MORNING, a gunfight broke out in a residential neighborhood in Kandahar, not far from my hotel. At first, people said that it was a confrontation between Mullah Naquib and Gul Agha, but it turned out that one of Gul Agha's commanders, who claimed that he hadn't been paid his salary, had led his soldiers on a robbery expedition, and the local police chief had foiled it. Things had been resolved by sunset, when I stopped by the governor's palace. The commander had barricaded himself in a police station and threatened to blow himself up with grenades, but he had finally surrendered. He and his men had been beaten and put in jail, a guard at the palace told me.

Gul Agha was receiving visitors in a long room that had a red carpet and chandeliers. A framed portrait of King Zahir Shah was propped on a desk at one end of the room. Four or five uniformed soldiers carrying rifles stood around, and a couple of dozen venerable-looking petitioners sat attentively on red sofas awaiting their turn to speak with the governor.

Gul Agha is a squat, bushy-haired man with a big belly and a rubbery face. He wore a brown *shalwar kameez* and sandals, and I noticed that his toenails were long and untidy. He was sitting in a chair next to the door, talking to a group of Noorzai tribal elders from the western province of Farah, an eight-hour drive from Kandahar. They had come to see him because they were having problems with mujahideen who had recently arrived from Iran. Gul Agha smoked a Benson & Hedges Special Filter cigarette and listened to the elders, and when they had finished he told them that he was aware of what he termed, darkly, "the Iranian interference" in their province, and that President Karzai was also aware of it. The problem would be dealt with soon. Gul Agha lisps clumsily, as if his tongue were too big for his mouth. "Before now," he said loudly, "there were commanders with autonomous power. But now I am the overall commander of the whole area."

While Gul Agha was speaking, a soldier passed out cold cans of Pepsi-Cola to some of the guests. I took one and sipped it and then placed the can on the floor next to my feet, but almost immediately someone stuck his hand under my chair and grabbed it. I turned around and saw a soldier sitting on the carpet behind me, holding the Pepsi and snickering to a friend. I reached over and swiped it back.

When it was my turn to speak with the governor, I asked him to describe his role in recent events. He had been governor of Kandahar during Rabbani's tenure, although Mullah Naquib, as military commander, had more power than he did then. When the Taliban took over Kandahar in 1994, Gul Agha moved to Quetta, across the border in Pakistan. "I went into business," he said, "trading goods between Pakistan, Japan, the United Arab Emirates, and other countries. When the Taliban and Al Qaeda became strong in Afghanistan, I wrote three separate letters to Mullah Omar, advising him not to do what he was doing, because he'd bring disaster upon Afghanistan. When he didn't listen to us, we began to fight against him, just as we fought against the Russians. The Afghan people have a long history, more than five thousand years old, and they have never accepted foreign invaders and have always fought to resist them. We have told the UN and U.S. troops at the airport that they are here to stop the foreign interference."

Gul Agha then complained at length about how some foreign powers, namely Iran and Russia, were still meddling in Afghanistan by backing fundamentalist warlords, including former President Rabbani. "These men all have the ideology of the Muslim Brotherhood," Gul Agha said. They were trying to sabotage the interim government of Hamid Karzai by disseminating propaganda, sending their gunmen to his territory, and generally stirring up trouble. "We want an end to foreign interference in Afghanistan," he repeated. "We want peace in Afghanistan and we ask Allah to help us have honest government. We want rights for women, and we are against drugs and terrorism. My greatest hope and wish is that there will be a broad-based government in Afghanistan without friction between different groups."

The governor sat back in his chair, apparently satisfied with his oration.

Since he had brought up the subject of friction, I said, what was his current relationship with Mullah Naquib?

"Mullah Naquib himself agreed to leave the government," Gul Agha replied, "and he has no duties now." He said that he had told Hamid Karzai that he did not want to work with Naquib. "It was he who brought the Taliban and Al Qaeda to Kandahar," Gul Agha said, and he had helped the Taliban leaders escape. "The world is not happy with him, and the Americans are not happy with him. So maybe he will be brought to justice."

AHMED WALI KARZAI, one of the president's younger brothers, lives in Kandahar, in a heavily guarded house a few miles from the governor's palace. He speaks fluent American-accented English. "I spent ten years in Chicago," he explained. "I opened the first Afghan restaurant there." His Chicago restaurant was one of a family-owned chain of Afghan restaurants in the United States, all of them called the Helmand, after Afghanistan's longest river.

"We're trying to get things functioning here again," Karzai said. "Our main concern is security. We want to get the gunmen off the streets, and we've asked the commanders to have no more than one or two bodyguards." Karzai was reasonably sanguine about the town rivals, Mullah Naquib and Gul Agha. It was just a matter of keeping a lid on things until international peacekeeping forces took over and an Afghan national army was in place.

Karzai was less circumspect about Naquib's relationship with the Taliban. "In the early days, we did kind of help the Taliban," he said. "But you have to understand that in the beginning they were mostly commanders who had fought against the Russians. There weren't any Arabs and only a few Pakistanis." The Karzais began campaigning against the Taliban a little over three years ago. "In July 1998, my brother and I talked to Mullah Naquib and asked him to go to Bonn"—for a meeting of Afghan opposition leaders— "and even gave him a ticket and a passport, but he didn't go," Karzai said. "He didn't want to leave his land, and he said that if he were to go to Bonn he would not be safe in Kandahar afterward. And I think this was the truth. But the fact is Naquib never took any action against the Taliban."

In November, when Gul Agha was approaching Kandahar from the south and Hamid Karzai was north of the city, Mullah Naquib was given the satellite phone to help him get involved. "But he said he was under too much surveillance," Ahmed Wali Karzai recalled. "All he did in the end was arrange for the talks between the Taliban and my brother. Mullah Naquib called me in Quetta to say that Mullah Omar was ready to talk." Karzai said that it was the Taliban's idea to hand the city over to Naquib. "But it didn't happen the way it had been agreed. We expected them to stay in the city, although we never expected Mullah Omar to remain."

Karzai said that the assassination attempt that had almost killed Naquib in 1998 had been ordered by the Taliban security chief. They had done an investigation and had evidence to prove it. An influential businessman in Kandahar told me the same thing and claimed that the Taliban flew Naquib to Pakistan for medical treatment in one of their own helicopters to cover up their complicity in the attempted murder. Why, I asked the businessman, would the Taliban have wanted to kill Naquib? "Because Naquib was the only powerful figure remaining in Kandahar from the time before the Taliban came," he said. "In Argandhab, the people consider him their tribal leader. He represented a potential threat to the Taliban."

The Taliban may have had reservations about Mullah Naquib, but in December, when they realized they had to leave the city, they turned to him to make the arrangements. A man named Khairullah, an intellectual in his sixties who is a distinguished elder in one of the city's tribal councils, told me that the Taliban had bequeathed Naquib many of their weapons when they left. Naquib had complained to me that Rabbani had withheld weapons from him, yet he seemed to have them now, and was vague about where they came from, just as he was vague about the acquisition of the ten Toyota Land Cruisers. Khairullah also said that, as far as he knew, Naquib didn't have any serious health problems, mental or otherwise—certainly nothing incapacitating.

ONE AFTERNOON, a man waiting outside Gul Agha's palace approached my translator, Qias, and said he had an Al Qaeda prisoner to sell. He was holding him in his house and would hand him over for two thousand dollars. Qias came back to our hotel to give me the news. He was excited. "What do you think?" he said. "What should I tell him? Will you pay the two thousand dollars?" I reminded Qias that I was not a Green Beret or a CIA agent. Where would I keep an Al Qaeda prisoner? But I was curious, so I told Qias to tell the man to come see me. He showed up a couple of hours later, and Qias went downstairs to talk to him. It turned out that the man's story had been a lie, bait to see if we were interested. He didn't actually have a prisoner in his house. He had come from a village in eastern Afghanistan about a day's drive away, where, he claimed, there were a hundred or so Al Qaeda fighters hiding in a nearby cave. The villagers sympathized with them and took turns taking them food and other supplies. He had delivered food to the cave himself a few days earlier. But he was willing to betray the men for two thousand dollars. He would guide us to the exact spot, so we could capture them, he said. Qias invited the man up to my room, but when Qias said that I was a journalist the deal was off. The man didn't want to talk to a journalist. He wanted to do business. In that case, Qias said, the best thing for him to do was to go out to the Kandahar airport and approach the Americans stationed there, who ran a detention camp for Al Qaeda members. The man thanked Qias and left.

I had been offered purloined Al Qaeda documents in Kabul and Jalalabad, and it didn't seem odd that an enterprising man from a village in eastern Afghanistan had raised the level of entrepreneurship. He must have assumed that if the Americans would pay twenty-five million dollars for Osama bin Laden they would pay a fair price for lesser souls.

Afghanistan was teeming with opportunists. It was not the country I had visited more than a decade earlier, when Mullah Naquib and his men were fighting a rather simple war over ideas of faith and nationhood. Or perhaps it just seemed simple then. Perhaps the jockeying for power, the hypocrisy and naked ambition and mendacity, had just not had a chance to flower.

I asked Qias what it would take for me to set myself up as a warlord in Afghanistan. "It would be easy," he said. "You hire a hundred gunmen for a month, get a few Toyota pickups, and you're in business." He estimated that it would cost about ten thousand dollars. Gunmen came cheap, and most of them had their own Kalashnikovs already. In any case, Kalashnikovs were cheap, too. We might, he suggested, spend a bit more to add some muscle. We could buy a few RPG rocket launchers and a heavy PK machine gun or two, for instance.

OK, I said. But once I have this army, what do I do? It is cheap enough to get going, but how do you sustain it?

This was also easy, Qias said. "In the first month, you find ways to make money so that it doesn't cost you anything more." You went to wealthy local people, merchants and traders, and asked them for money, and they paid.

Qias seemed to be talking about setting up a protection racket. Extortion was only the beginning, of course, he explained. Most of the mujahideen commanders in the Northern Alliance, for instance, were also involved in the opium and heroin trade.

Qias is young, maybe twenty-two, and his enthusiasm for whatever enterprise presents itself to him will serve him well in the new Afghanistan, just as Naquib's pragmatism and canny methods of dealing with the authorities have enabled him to prosper and to survive sudden and dangerous shifts in power. I even began to wonder about Naquib's illness, which conveniently removed him from a confrontation with Gul Agha that he probably wouldn't have won. His Risperdal capsules reminded me of Vincent (the Chin) Gigante, shuffling around Greenwich Village in his bathrobe and pajamas, trying to avoid racketeering charges. But then perhaps I had been in Afghanistan too long.

From: Jon Lee 2/19/2002
Re returning to Afghanistan. I am assuming that a trip there for the magazine is in order sooner rather than later. Sometime in April is probably the time to go. A profile of Karzai is one idea for a focus. Or a Letter from Kabul, which would take in what has happened on the ground since I left: peacekeeping troops, various foreign powers involved in reconstruction. And of course there is the return of the king and the upcoming Loya Jirga.

From: Jon Lee 3/20/2002
I have my Afghan and Pakistani visas and will be getting my hepatitis A booster, etc. Will have my cell phone with me.

From: Jon Lee 3/22/2002
I'll be seeing Wali Massoud in London on Tuesday and have been thinking more about Ahmed Massoud's murder. Could a proper look into it be something I might do? This might be the peg for a story about the Taliban–Al Qaeda assassination campaign against potential or real opposition leaders in recent years. Karzai's father was murdered in Kandahar in '98, I think. Abdul Haq's entire family was murdered in Peshawar (and then, of course, they hung him in

October). There was also the hit on Mullah Naquib in '98. There was a definite pattern of murders carried out by Al Qaeda on behalf of the Taliban in the two or three years before September 11.

From: Jon Lee 4/2/2002
Wali has slipped the noose. He's been in meetings constantly. I've left numerous messages and asked the secretary to get a fixed hour and day this week for me. No news yet. I have the sat phone set up with a signal but it's not communicating with my laptop modem. I'm trying to figure out what's up. It's just one bloody thing after another.

From: Jon Lee 4/4/2002
I have my Indian visa, my ticket, and I'm seeing Wali at four. He is rushing to leave for Kabul too and has a lot of official appointments but is squeezing me in. I shall make as much of it as I can and will try to pin him down for next week.

From: Jon Lee 4/5/2002
I got Thomas's money (minus ten percent!!!!) after an incredible exchange fiddle at Western Union. I'm out of here.

From: Jon Lee 4/7/2002
Hi. Made it to New Delhi late last night. Thomas was waiting. It is dust season and the sky has a surreal quality. It's dry and hot and there are cows walking through traffic. Will give you a call early afternoon your time. If all goes well, we leave at daylight for Kabul. All best.

From: Jon Lee 4/9/2002
Arrived in Kabul at the newly renamed Ahmed Shah Massoud International Airport yesterday on the Ariana flight from New Delhi. We got to the airport at 5:30 A.M. and were finally allowed on the

plane—a vintage Boeing 727 with all the luggage piled onto the seats and aisles at the rear—at 2:30 P.M. The plane took off at 4:15. It turned out that we were waiting for the Indian authorities to deliver the body of a man who had died on the incoming Ariana flight the previous day. His tearful brother, a half-blind bearded man from Badakhshan, sat next to us. The dead man was coming to India for medical treatment, but he didn't make it.

The weather is springlike, cool and breezy, and there is actually green on top of the brown sod. But the mountains ringing Kabul are still covered with snow. We've been put up, thanks to Thomas's friend Yuri, in the LA Times house. They put on a nice dinner for us, and we had hot showers and slept like logs. Waiting to see whether the other LA Times guys here are OK with us staying or if we should find our own place.

There are women on the streets now without burkhas. The city seems cleaner. The streets have been swept, and they are emptier than I remember. There are still some beggars, and lots of traffic, but it moves in an orderly fashion that is unusual for Afghanistan. You see patrols of German and British troops here and there.

Spent much of the middle part of the day over at the now brimming and busy Mustafa Hotel, which is run by the Afghan New Jerseyite brothers Weiss and Salomon. A lot of hacks were sitting around reading novels or trying to talk on their Thuraya sat phones. Had a late breakfast with Steve Connors, who has become the longest-staying hack in Afghanistan. He told us stories about the area around Khost, where there is a shrine built by the locals to commemorate the Talibs and Qaeda guys killed in a mosque by the Americans. Peter Jouvenal's house is supposed to be the guest house to stay in, but is always full; a badminton court, a sun room, and so forth. Peter is said to be setting up a Correspondent's Club.

There was a bombing attempt on Fahim's life yesterday in Jalalabad. And Sayyaf's men are said to be robbing and murdering Hazaras in western Kabul. A British soldier was shot in the head today. It was perhaps an accident, and it is not known whether he is dead or not. This took place as the hacks were out there reporting on the troops' Queen Mum remembrance ceremony.

From: Jon Lee 4/13/2002
You can try calling me on the Thuraya, since I have it on most of the time, and with me. Sometimes, especially indoors, I am out of range, but I think that you can leave messages.

From: Jon Lee 4/14/2002
I may get a chip for my cell phone, which will provide another communcations option. I notice that the Thuraya often goes to "No Network" if I am moving around, which means that it's kind of a shot in the dark if you try to call me.

From: Jon Lee 4/15/2002
It rained all day yesterday and most of the night, and around one in the morning there was a huge explosionlike jolt with aftershocks that made everything shake. I gather that it was an earthquake.

From: Jon Lee 4/19/2002
Weird weather here. This afternoon, suddenly, there was an invasion of flies. Then, around dusk, flashes of sheet lightning, and tonight strange, strong winds and the sound of choppers overhead. Closer to hand, what sound awfully like big rats seem to be running through the rafters. The chopper has just come right over the house and its clatter is deafening. Now it's gone, but the flies are still here. This is especially disconcerting and rather millennial-feeling, since it's after curfew and the city is deserted.

From: Jon Lee 4/29/2002
The house we've taken is in the central district of Sharinaw, on Flower Street, fifty meters from an NGO that operates the Emergency Surgical Centre for War Victims. Our front door lies directly

across from a shop that makes AK-47 ammunition belts. It is easy to find, because the ammo belts hang over the sidewalk outside the shop. The house is Afghan in design. Basically it is a long, three-sided structure of contiguous rooms wrapped around a central courtyard. The courtyard has a small stone patio and rose bushes and a newly planted lawn with a well in the middle. We now have nine songbirds in cages, which Thomas brought back one day from the bazaar. They tweeter away, and are visited by wild birds which flit around and sing along with them. We also have a three-and-a-half-foot mock F-16 jet fighter made out of a tank shell and antiaircraft bullets, painted green, which Thomas also found in the bazaar and brought home. It is aimed toward the front door.

At one end of the house, there is a little cubicle for the night watchmen, of whom we have two, who rotate shifts. Then there is the kitchen, with a door to another room, where one of our two translators, Qias, sleeps. It has an adjoining WC, and next to it, a shower. Then there are three rooms in a row, one of which, with its own entrance to the patio, is mine. There is another bedroom between me and the main hall, and then a large common room where we eat our meals, and then Thomas's room—which is decorated with anatomical dissection charts from Kabul's medical school—and, finally, the main bathroom. The cement floors of our rooms are all covered with brown carpeting. There are a few beds, but mostly red-velveteen-covered sleeping cushions filled with raw cotton, and matching cushions.

Our electricity supply is fairly constant because we pay the equivalent of a five-dollar-a-week bribe to the local man in charge. (I am not sure how this works, but the landlord told us this is what everyone around here does.) The plumbing is not good. We have hot water, but the landlord and his minions are constantly coming around to tinker with the well, or our toilets, which tend not to flush, or else overflow.

If you walk down Flower Street in the opposite direction from the Emergency Centre, you soon come to a gaggle of florists and several wedding-decoration shops. There is usually a car or two outside on the sidewalk being carefully festooned with wedding flowers and ribbons by fastidious, formally dressed shop attendants. After the wedding shops there is a half-block of food stores, stocked with imported packaged or tinned goods smuggled in from Pakistan and sold at huge markups. Flower Street turns into Chicken Street across the next main avenue. Years ago, Chicken Street was where people bought their eggs, but since the sixties, when European hippies began hanging out in Kabul between pilgrimages to Kathmandu, it has been the central shopping street for ethnic goods. It is now a block-long lane of carpet dealers, antiquarians, and furriers. Shop fronts are festooned with wolfskin coats, leopard skins, karakul hats, old muskets and knives, carpets from Herat and Mazar-i-Sharif, and the popular Afghan war rugs, which are decorated with images of MiG fighters, helicopter gunships, and Kalashnikov assault rifles. Jeeps belonging to ISAF, the international peacekeeping forces, are usually parked all along Chicken Street. The locals joke that the brawny men dressed in civilian clothes and carrying weapons who are apparently U.S. Special Forces spend all their time shopping rather than chasing bin Laden, and that they pay ridiculous prices for things.

From: Jon Lee 5/11/2002

Thanks to the influx of free-spending Westerners, a newly monied class of Afghans is emerging. Real-estate agents, translators, food importers, and carpet dealers are making money hand over fist. A number of car dealers have opened up for business, offering new and used Toyota Hi-Lux pickups and Land Cruisers, which are shipped in from the duty-free zone of Dubai through Iran. All over Kabul, battered, bombed-out, and decrepit residential homes, which have been sitting vacant for years, are being repaired. In some cases, it is so that their owners, returning from exile, can live in them again, but they are often rented out at fantastically high prices to foreigners. I was shown several large houses in the choice district of Wazir Akbar Khan, and the rent being asked for them, unfurnished and in various states of dilapidation, ranged from between five and seven thousand dollars a month.

Pakistani border authorities are said to be demanding higher bribes than usual from the Afghan refugees who are flooding back to the country. The relative of one friend who returned recently was ordered to pay a thousand Pakistani rupees instead of the customary one hundred to cross the border. When he asked why, the border official told him: "Because it's raining dollars in Kabul now, and you'll soon be rich."

Even a few tourists have begun to pitch up. One afternoon in late April, a mysterious group of Japanese in casual clothing were spotted taking photographs and shooting home movies at the destroyed hilltop tomb of King Nadir Shah, Zahir Shah's father.

Alcohol has made a comeback, although a British friend brought some cans of beer to our house one evening only to discover that they bore an expiration date of 1989, the year of the Russian military withdrawal from Afghanistan. Heroin, opium, and hashish are available, too. Wazir Akbar Khan, which is where most journalists, diplomats, and relief-agency expats live, is referred to by the locals as Kafiristan, and at parties there, spiked punch flows and techno and rock and hip-hop music blare from stereos.

Perhaps one of the most telling signs of change in Kabul is the expanding English vocabulary of Kabul's street beggars, women in soiled blue burkhas and groups of pushy young girls and boys. A few months ago, their lexicon consisted of not much more than persistent cries of: "Baksheesh, Mister." Now, when they are spurned, some have learned to yell, repeatedly and with near-perfect inflection, "Fuck you!"

Security has improved. There are still plenty of men with guns, and mujahideen too, but since the ISAF's appearance on the scene,

they have been better behaved. Razorwire, video cameras, and high
walls protect the foreign embassies, most of which were vacant at
the end of last year but have now reopened for business. The U.S.
embassy is the most heavily guarded place in town. Huge steel plates
have been put along the rock wall that surrounds the legation, and
flakjacketed and helmeted marines sit watchfully in sandbagged
machine-gun nests. There was a security briefing for American journalists at the embassy in early May. They were warned that terrorist cells could become active in the city this summer and that
journalists were especially vulnerable to attack. Evacuation procedures have been put in place for U.S. citizens, and all Americans in
the country have been advised to register with the embassy for this
contingency. Afghans, too, believe there may be terrorist attacks
soon. A friend with close ties to the Afghan intelligence service
warned me that he had been advised that an assassination team
composed of Afghans but acting on behalf of Al Qaeda had recently
arrived in Kabul from Pakistan. The identity of the leader of the cell
was known and also the number of men he had brought with him;
only their intended targets, and their whereabouts, were a mystery.

The Assassins

A hmed Shah Massoud was a wiry, thin-boned man with
a long, handsome face that was distinguished by an
aquiline nose and by deep furrows in the cheeks and
around the eyes. He had a patchy beard at the edge of his
jawline. He usually wore a *pakul,* a kind of flat-topped, soft
wool hat, which he and his mujahideen had adopted from
the Nuristani, a tribe that claims to have descended from
Alexander the Great's army. In the fall of last year, Massoud
was forty-nine years old, and dramatic white streaks had
appeared in his dark hair, above his temples.

Massoud had been at war pretty much steadily since
1975, when he and several other anti-Communist Islamist
students made a series of botched attacks on outposts of
the government of Muhammad Daoud. In the fall of 2001,
he had been fighting the Taliban for more than five years,
and his front line by then extended from the edge of the
Shamali plain, which lies between the Panjshir Valley and
Kabul, for about a hundred and eighty miles, up to the
Tajik border, where he had his headquarters in Khoja
Bahauddin, a little smugglers' town.

That summer, Massoud had begun receiving intelligence reports that a large number of Taliban and Al Qaeda
fighters, as many as sixteen thousand, were massing along
his northernmost front, among them many Arabs, Pakistanis, Chinese, Uzbeks, and Tajiks. These numbers seemed
preposterously inflated, and he dismissed them. Early in
September, he and several of his commanders flew over the
front line in a helicopter. Massoud sat in the cockpit with
binoculars. It was a dangerous trip, one of the men who was
with him recalled recently, "but we knew that Allah would
help us and that Amur Sahib"—a phrase meaning, more or
less, Big Boss, which is what Massoud's men called him—
"was with us." They photographed the area, and Massoud
instructed his commanders where to position their men.

Massoud stayed up reading Persian poetry aloud with
several colleagues until three in the morning on September 9th. A few minutes after he went to sleep, his personal
secretary—a young man named Jamshid, who was also his
nephew and his brother-in-law—received a call from a
Northern Alliance commander, Bismillah Khan, saying
that the Taliban had attacked the Shamali front. Jamshid
woke Massoud up, and Massoud and Bismillah Khan talked
on the phone until daybreak. Then Massoud went back to
bed. Around seven-thirty, Jamshid learned that the Taliban
were in retreat, and he let his uncle sleep until nine.

After breakfast, Massoud was about to leave on a re-
connaissance trip when he decided to see two Arab journalists who had come to Khoja Bahauddin from the
Panjshir Valley nine days earlier and had been waiting to
interview him. They had sent word that they had to leave
Khoja Bahauddin that day. The Arabs had arrived with a
letter of introduction from the director of an organization

called the Islamic Observation Centre, in London. Jamshid says that he was also contacted by a man who worked for Abdul Rasul Sayyaf, one of the founders of the Afghan Islamist movement, who now commanded a thousand-odd anti-Taliban fighters from a base in the Panjshir. Jamshid was told that the Arabs were friends of Sayyaf's.

I asked Jamshid if he had noticed anything unusual about the Arabs, since most Arabs in Afghanistan at the time were associated with Al Qaeda. "No," he said. And his uncle thought they could be of use. "He wanted to say through them to the Muslim world, 'We are not *kafirs*. We are Muslims, and we don't have Russians and Iranians fighting here.' " Massoud was religious. He prayed five times a day, in the orthodox fashion, and his wife wore a burkha. But he was a Sunni Muslim at war with other Sunni Muslims—the Taliban—and they professed to be righteous and incorruptible, while he had accepted support from Iranian Shiites and from non-Muslim governments.

Fahim Dashty, a slender young man who is now the editor of a multilingual newspaper in Kabul, was also in Khoja Bahauddin on September 9. Dashty had known Massoud since he was a small boy. In the fall of 1996, when the Taliban took Kabul, Dashty joined Massoud's retreat to the Panjshir Valley. He stayed in Northern Alliance territory and formed a small film company, Ariana, with one of Massoud's commanders. They made documentaries about Massoud's war with the Taliban. Dashty had just come back from a two-month stay in Paris, where he participated in a workshop on film editing sponsored by the group Reporters Without Borders. He stayed in the same guest house as the two Arabs. He remembers thinking that it was odd to see Arabs in Northern Alliance territory, but that these two didn't seem suspicious. "They had gone to refugee camps, and to visit prisoners—all the things journalists do," he said. One of them spoke a little French and English, the other only Arabic.

A few weeks ago, I was shown a rough cut of Ariana's most recent film about Massoud. The two Arabs are in some of the scenes. In footage shot in August, they are interviewing Burhanuddin Rabbani. The putative reporter is a fair-skinned, muscular man who appears to be in his mid-thirties. He is clean-shaven and has a crewcut. He wears Western clothes—a brown shirt and slacks—and glasses. He has two odd brownish marks, like round scars, on his forehead. The cameraman isn't visible in this scene, but later in the film there is a still shot of him in the doorway of the guest house. He is tall and dark-skinned. He is wearing a black shirt and is glaring at the camera, with what one can easily imagine is both hatred and fear.

The Ariana team usually filmed Massoud's interviews, and around noon on September 9th Fahim Dashty and the two Arabs and their translator drove over to Massoud's headquarters. Massoud and Jamshid were there with the chief of security, whose office was being used for the interview, and Massoud Khalili, the Northern Alliance's ambassador to India. Ahmed Shah Massoud was sitting on a sofa, using an orthopedic cushion that helped alleviate his chronic back pain. He said hello to the Arabs. "He asked them where they were from," Dashty said. "One of them said they were Belgian but were born in Morocco, and that they had come from Pakistan to Kabul and from there to Khoja Bahauddin."

Ambassador Khalili recalled that Massoud told the Arab who was to conduct the interview that he would like to hear the list of questions first, and the man began to read them out in English. Khalili translated into Persian for Massoud. He said that he was rather surprised that most of the questions had to do with Osama bin Laden— for example, "What will you do with Osama bin Laden if you take power?" and "Why do you call him a fundamentalist?" The ambassador found the questions tendentious, and he asked the Arab what paper he worked for. "I am not a journalist," the man replied. "I am from the Islamic centers. We have offices in London and Paris and all over the world." Khalili turned to Massoud and whispered, "Commander, they are from those guys"—meaning Al Qaeda. Massoud nodded, and said, tersely, "Let's just get through with it."

The Arabs had moved a table and some chairs that were between Massoud and their camera, which they had positioned on the lowest level of the tripod. Dashty, who had set up his camera behind theirs, was adjusting his backlight when the room exploded. Ambassador Khalili said that he saw a thick blue fire coming toward him.

"I felt I was burning," Dashty said. He went outside and saw Jamshid, who had left the room with the chief of security a few minutes earlier. "I asked him to take me to the hospital, and he asked me where Mr. Massoud was, and I went back inside and saw him. He was very badly injured all over his body, his face, his hands and legs." An Afghan intelligence officer told me recently that Massoud must have died within thirty seconds. Two pieces of metal were lodged in his heart. Most of the fingers of his right hand had been blown off. I was shown a photograph of his body. Every other inch of his skin was ruptured in open wounds. White gauze had been stuffed into his eye sockets.

The cameraman's battery belt had been packed with explosives. The sofa that Massoud had been sitting on was charred, and a hole had been blasted through the back. In the Ariana film, there is a shot of the cameraman's body on a stretcher. His legs are scorched and bloody and the upper part of his body seems to have been blown apart. The Afghan translator was also killed.

Two bodyguards carried Massoud to his car. Dashty, who was badly burned, got in, and they drove to the helicopter pad. Ambassador Khalili, who was also burned and had been hit heavily by shrapnel, followed in another car. They were all flown to a hospital across the border in Tajikistan, where General Fahim, Massoud's second-in-command, soon arrived. Fahim conferred with other Northern Alliance officials, and they agreed that the assassination should be kept a secret for the time being.

The Arab who did the interviewing had survived the blast, and while Massoud's body was being taken to Tajikistan, he was held in a room near where the explosion had taken place. He tore the wire-mesh screen from a small window and wriggled through, then ran across a graveyard to a steep river embankment a few hundred yards away. A man who worked for a local warlord chased him and killed him.

I asked Dashty if he believed that Massoud had been betrayed. "Yes," he said. "It would have been impossible otherwise. Somehow, I think, there was contact between Al Qaeda and our guys."

ON SEPTEMBER 11TH, at around 8 P.M. in Afghanistan, Mullah Omar, who was in Kandahar, called the Taliban foreign minister in Kabul. According to Afghan intelligence sources, who intercepted the call, Mullah Omar said, "Things have gone much further than expected." It was 11:30 A.M. in New York, less than three hours after American Airlines Flight 11 had crashed into the north tower of the World Trade Center, and an hour and a half after the south tower had collapsed. Mullah Omar told the foreign minister to call a press conference to say that the Taliban had not been involved in the attack. The press conference took place at 9:30 P.M. in Kabul. The foreign minister assured reporters that Afghanistan had not attacked the United States, and he read a statement by Mullah Omar saying that Osama bin Laden was not involved: "This type of terrorism is too great for one man."

Among the calls intercepted that night was one from Kabul to Kandahar. "Where's the Sheikh?" the caller asked. Sheikh was the code name that senior Taliban officials used for Osama bin Laden. Again according to Afghan intelligence sources, someone in Mullah Omar's house told the caller that bin Laden was there. "Then, afterward," an intelligence officer said to me, "there was a chaos of phone calls back and forth between Kandahar and Kabul."

It seemed obvious during those early days in September that the assassination of Massoud on the ninth and the attack on the World Trade Center two days later were somehow related, but exactly how they were related and who was involved continues to be the subject of speculation. Massoud's younger brother, Wali, who was the chargé d'affaires at the Afghan embassy in London when Massoud was killed, is now in Kabul, and has been nominated to lead a Massoudist party, the National Movement of Afghanistan. He believes that the assassination of his brother was the first step in a larger plot, and that the attacks on September 11th were the second step. "Look at the logic," he says. "They wanted to do what they wanted to do on the eleventh, but provided there was no Massoud." The people who killed Massoud assumed that his death would destroy the Northern Alliance, and that if the Americans retaliated for the attacks on the World Trade Center they would have no Afghan allies on the ground. The buildup of troops on the front lines in the late summer and early fall was, then, preparation for Massoud's assassination. "They were waiting for something," an Afghan intelligence official said. The foreign troops that were prepared to overrun a demoralized Northern Alliance were, it appears, to have marched into Central Asia. In the ensuing chaos, reprisals against Osama bin Laden and the Taliban would have been difficult. But since the official story was, at first, that Massoud had only been wounded, the Northern Alliance held its ground. And, of course, as can be seen from Mullah Omar's phone conversation, the operation against the United States was not expected to be as spectacular as it turned out to be. "They were expecting a reaction," the intelligence official said. "But they thought it would be a Clinton-type reaction. They didn't anticipate the kind of revenge that occurred."

The "terrorists," which is the word that Afghans commonly use to refer to Al Qaeda, had strategic as well as tactical reasons for wanting to kill Massoud. Their most stalwart enemy had begun to gain support outside the country. In April 2001, Massoud had been invited to speak to the European Parliament in Strasbourg. He gave a press conference in Paris and met with European officials there and in Brussels. "He behaved like a statesman and was received as a statesman," Wali says. "The media took an interest in him—except for the American media. I think this was a turning point. He warned the international community that Al Qaeda was dangerous, not only to Afghanistan but to the world." In July, in London, Wali organized a conference of Afghan intellectuals in exile. They passed a resolution endorsing Massoud and various motions in support of democracy, human rights, and women's rights. "This spurred his enemies against him," Wali said. "On the one side there was Osama, saying, 'We represent Muslims,' and on the other Massoud, who stood for moderate Islam. That trip to Europe, in which he outlined his vision, cost him his life."

Wali and other Afghans I talked to insisted that Pakistan was also involved in Massoud's murder. Massoud had never established close links with the Pakistanis, even in the seventies and eighties, when many Afghan Islamists went into exile in Pakistan. (He was legendary as a fighter in part because he stayed in Afghanistan, in the field.) The I.S.I., the Pakistani security services, had supported the Taliban early on, and many people suspect that the remnants of the Taliban and Al Qaeda are still getting assistance from Pakistan. An intelligence officer who was close to Massoud said that on the night of September 9th the president of Pakistan, Pervez Musharraf, held a party to celebrate the assassination. He said that this information came from General Fahim, who is now minister of defense in the interim Afghan government headed by Hamid Karzai. I asked Fahim if there had been such a party, and he was evasive. "Maybe," he said. But he confirmed that Musharraf was at I.S.I. headquarters that evening, meeting with Hamid Gul, the former head of the I.S.I., who had just returned from northern Afghanistan. I asked Fahim what he felt when he met Musharraf recently in Kabul. He had shaken his hand. "Sometimes, for the sake of the greater interest," Fahim said, "one has to take a cup of poison."

MASSOUD'S ASSASSINS WERE TUNISIANS, not Moroccans, as they had claimed. They had been in Belgium, and they carried Belgian passports and letters of introduction with the signature of Yassir al-Sirri, the director of the Islamic Observation Centre. The stamps on the passports indicated that the Arabs had arrived in Islamabad, Pakistan, on July 25, where they were given visas by the Taliban embassy, and that they went from there to Kabul. But the passports and visas were forged. Both of the assassins had been living for several months in an Al Qaeda training camp near Jalalabad.

The assassins entered the Panjshir Valley under the auspices of the Northern Alliance leader Abdul Rasul Sayyaf, who says that in mid-August he was contacted by an Egyptian who had fought with him in the jihad against the Soviets. The man said that he was calling from Bosnia. (Although an Afghan intelligence officer told me that the call had, in fact, come from Kandahar.) The man asked Sayyaf to help two Arab journalists who wanted to interview him and Massoud and President Rabbani. Engineer Muhammad Aref ("engineer" is a common Afghan honorific, indicating that someone is educated and has studied engineering), who is now the head of the Afghan intelligence services, was Massoud's chief of security; it was in his office that the assassination took place. Aref says that Sayyaf's imprimatur permitted the Arabs to bypass normal security procedures. "They came not as journalists but as guests," Aref says. "Sayyaf and Bismillah Khan"—the commander of the Shamali front line—"sent their men and cars to pick them up. Everybody helped them, and they met lots of people."

Maulana Attah Rahman Salim, a deputy minister in Karzai's interim government, is a respected Muslim scholar and cleric. He had an office in Khoja Bahauddin last fall and travelled to the Panjshir Valley with Massoud a week before the assassination. Rahman says that recriminations were voiced almost immediately after Massoud was killed. "Everyone began saying, 'Why weren't the terrorists searched more carefully? Why didn't people do their jobs better?' The accusations focused on Sayyaf more than anyone else, and an Iranian newspaper published the suspicions."

Sayyaf is an Islamic fundamentalist and is closely associated with the global terrorists who were nurtured during the Afghan jihad in the eighties. He and Rabbani studied at al-Azhar University in Cairo, where they were influenced by the Muslim Brotherhood, and they both taught Islamic studies at Kabul University in the early seventies. They were among the founders of the Islamist movement that became the principal opposition to the Soviets. Sayyaf, who is a Pashtun, spoke Arabic fluently, and he became close to the Saudis. Like the Saudi royal family, he is a member of the severe Wahabbi sect, and after the Communist takeover of Afghanistan in the late seventies, when the Saudis began to fund various Afghan resistance movements, Sayyaf received an inordinate share of the largesse. He formed a political party, the Ittihad-i-Islami, or Islamic Union, in 1981, and four years later founded a university in an Afghan refugee camp near Peshawar. He was allied politically with

Massoud and Rabbani, but in many ways he has more in common ideologically with the Islamists who became the Taliban.

Sayyaf's university was called Dawa'a al-Jihad, which means Convert and Struggle, and it became known as the preeminent "school for terrorism." Ramzi Ahmed Yousef, who is serving a life sentence in a federal prison in Colorado for masterminding the bombing of the World Trade Center in 1993, attended Dawa'a al-Jihad and fought with Sayyaf's mujahideen. Sheikh Omar Abdel-Rahman, the blind Egyptian cleric who is in the same prison, serving a life sentence for seditious conspiracy to blow up various New York City landmarks (not including the World Trade Center, although he is suspected of having been involved in the first bombing of that, too), lectured in the camps around Peshawar in the mid-eighties. Osama bin Laden supported Sayyaf financially and led a brigade of Arab fighters who used Sayyaf's base in Afghanistan. The I.S.I. provided military and intelligence expertise. When the Soviets withdrew from Afghanistan in 1989 and many of the foreign jihadis moved on, a group of Ittihad members—some of them native Filipinos and some of them Arabs—formed the Abu Sayyaf terrorist organization in the Philippines.

In October 2001, Yassir al-Sirri, of the Islamic Observation Centre, was arrested in London for his alleged role in the preparation of the letters of introduction for the two Arab assassins. In April, 2002, in New York, Ahmed Abdel Sattar, a U.S. Postal Service employee who lives on Staten Island, was arrested and charged with being a "surrogate" for Sheikh Omar Abdel-Rahman. Sattar had worked for the sheikh as a paralegal during his conspiracy trial in New York in the mid-nineties. The indictment said that Sattar was serving as a "communications facility" for the sheikh—

that is, passing on his orders from jail. Sattar's phone had
been tapped for some time, and among the calls scrutinized
were several between him and Yassir al-Sirri in London. In
May, a British judge dismissed the charges against al-Sirri.

ABDUL RASUL SAYYAF is a big, beefy man with fair skin and a
thick gray beard. He must be about six foot three and
weighs probably two hundred and fifty pounds. He usually
wears a white skullcap or a large turban and a *shalwar
kameez*. Wali Massoud is slight and clean-shaven. He usually wears slacks and a sports jacket. His dark hair is parted
on one side, and it often flops about boyishly. On April 28th,
during a parade in Kabul to commemorate the tenth anniversary of the mujahideen's entry into the city and their
victory over the Soviet-backed government there, Wali and
Sayyaf were sitting together on a V.I.P. viewing stand across
the street from the Eid Mosque, a long, low, pale-yellow-
and-green building with a yellow dome.

The V.I.Ps looked out over a Daliesque panorama of
wholesale destruction. Southern Kabul is a desolate ex-
panse of collapsed and gouged buildings, and most of the
jihadi leaders on the viewing stand had participated in the
destruction. Tens of thousands of people were slaughtered
in the internecine battles that took place between April
1992, when Ahmed Shah Massoud triumphantly entered
Kabul, and September 1996, when Massoud's forces retreated to the north and the Taliban took over. Most of the
men on the viewing stand were also now maneuvering for
position in the new government in Kabul, which would be
chosen at the Loya Jirga, the tribal council to be held six
weeks later. It was assumed that the Loya Jirga would

ratify Hamid Karzai as head of state. Wali could become
prime minister or vice president, which might appeal to
Karzai, since that arrangement would assure him the continued support of the Three Panjshiris—Defense Minister
Fahim, Foreign Minister Abdullah Abdullah, and Interior
Minister Yunis Qanouni—who grew up in the Panjshir
Valley and were close to Massoud, and are the leading figures in the new configuration of the old Northern Alliance
faction of ethnic Tajiks.

Karzai sat at the center of the front row of dignitar-
ies, in a gray silk collarless shirt and a gray *chapan,* a finely
woven Afghan robe. General Fahim was on his right, re-
splendent in a medal-bedecked uniform and peaked cap.
General Fahim was now officially Marshal Fahim, having
received a sudden promotion the night before. A number
of other mujahideen commanders loyal to Fahim had also
been promoted. (A few days later, I asked one of President
Karzai's Afghan-American advisers if the promotions were
Karzai's idea. "They forced him to do it," the man said. "He
had no choice." We were talking in a parking lot, because,
the adviser explained to me, the Intercontinental Hotel,
where he and several other members of Karzai's government live, is bugged: "They're in the curtains.")

Wali Massoud sat between Karzai and Sayyaf, and ex-
President Rabbani was on Sayyaf's other side, next to several other of the surviving jihadis. Among the missing
figures in the national drama were Gulbuddin Hekmatyar,
Massoud's archenemy, who had shelled the city merci-
lessly in the early nineties. Hekmatyar's whereabouts are
unknown, although two weeks after the parade there were
reports that the CIA had fired a missile at him from an
unmanned Predator spy plane, somewhere near Kabul. The

Uzbek warlord Rashid Dostum, who liberated much of the northern part of the country from the Taliban, did not attend. To do so would have been inappropriate, since Dostum fought on the Soviet side during the jihad. It had been thought that Zahir Shah, the former king, who had not been seen in public since his arrival in Kabul a week earlier, would make an appearance, but he didn't.

Patriotic music began blaring from loudspeakers, and Karzai and Fahim left the viewing stand and got into two convertible Russian military jeeps. The jeeps were driven past squads of soldiers who stood at attention in the great plaza in front of the mosque. Karzai waved at the soldiers and Fahim saluted stiffly, the tips of his fingers almost touching the beak of his outsized marshal's hat. Meanwhile, a master of ceremonies and a poet took turns at the microphone. "Whoever attacks Afghanistan will weep, just as Britain and Russia did," the master of ceremonies said. Karzai and Fahim returned to the viewing stand, and Fahim made a speech about how the mujahideen had vanquished the Soviets and the Taliban. He didn't mention the American bombing campaign. A float moved slowly down the avenue, bearing a huge portrait of Massoud in white safari clothes, his arms thoughtfully folded. Mujahideen holding Kalashnikovs stood at attention. Some of them wore Massoud T-shirts. Karzai announced that Massoud was henceforth Afghanistan's official National Hero.

Scores of Russian tanks and armored personnel carriers rumbled past bearing framed portraits of Massoud and Karzai. They were followed by disabled jihadi veterans in blue-gray tunics, on crutches and in wheelchairs. Behind the veterans came one marching platoon after another of

mujahideen, organized according to their home provinces, with Massoud's Panjshiris in the lead. A parachutist floated down from a helicopter, intending to land in front
of the mosque, but he missed his target and drifted off into
the ruins in the distance. Fifteen minutes later, he showed
up on the back of a motorbike, his parachute billowing behind him. A second parachutist, a woman this time, headed
for the plaza, and she, too, disappeared into the ruins but
soon reappeared, marching by to applause, and carrying a
carpet decorated with Massoud's image.

As the parade ended, I made my way past the front of
the viewing stand, close enough to see Sayyaf lean over and
say something to Wali Massoud. Wali sat bolt upright in
his chair. He nodded his head and smiled unconvincingly.

AFTER THE MEETING of Afghan delegations in Bonn in December 2001, at which Karzai's interim government was set up,
two of Sayyaf's deputies were given minor ministerial positions. Apparently, Sayyaf was reasonably happy with this
arrangement, and he agreed to withdraw his gunmen from
Kabul and to establish a command base in his hometown
of Paghman, an hour's drive into the mountains northwest
of the city. His militia controls all the territory between
Paghman and the suburbs of Kabul, ending just a few hundred metres from the Intercontinental Hotel.

In March, the I.S.A.F., the international security force
in Afghanistan, accused Sayyaf's militiamen of carrying out
several robberies and killings in the western suburbs,
where many of the city's minority ethnic Shia Muslims, the
Hazaras, live. Sayyaf denied the accusations. As with most
such incidents in Afghanistan, the investigation of this one
appears to have fizzled away inconclusively. There is a lot

of bad history between Sayyaf and the Hazaras. In the mid-nineties, Sayyaf's troops massacred perhaps thousands of Hazara civilians in Kabul. According to Human Rights Watch, his militia became renowned for a particularly gruesome method of dispatching its enemies—herding them into metal shipping containers and then setting fires beneath them, to roast them alive.

A medical student told me that he had studied under Sayyaf at the University of Kabul in 1996, before the Taliban took the city. Sayyaf taught a required course in Islamic thought. "He would arrive in a convoy of two or three cars with sixteen to twenty armed bodyguards," the young man recalled. "Some of the bodyguards would stay with the cars, others would stand at the doors, and two or three would stand next to him on the stage of a large hall. Sometimes, we could hear the sound of bombs and Kalashnikovs and RPG's while he was teaching us. We all knew that his men were fighting with the Hazara and that their positions were nearby. Sayyaf would say to us: 'In Islam it's forbidden to kill a Muslim, and it's forbidden to destroy and loot houses,' and then just a day or two later we would hear that his men had looted and destroyed a lot of houses and taken Hazara girls to their barracks. I heard that Sayyaf's men cut off women's breasts. None of us ever asked him about this, because we knew if we did, we'd be taken out of the classroom and killed.

"There were boys and girls in our classes," the young man said, "but they put up a curtain between us. The girls especially hated Sayyaf. One day he gave us some papers that talked about how in all the Muslim countries there were demonstrations in favor of Palestine and against Israel. 'Demonstrating cannot help Palestinians,' he said, 'because Palestinians cannot make weapons from our demonstrations to fight against Israel. Palestinians cannot make food from our demonstrations to eat, and Palestinians cannot use our demonstrations as a house to live in. We must help them directly, not just by demonstrating and shouting.' He never talked about the fighting that was going on then in Kabul.

"At that time, his Dawa'a al-Jihad university was in Kabul. He had brought it from Pakistan. It was in a building next to the Kabul Polytechnic, behind the Intercontinental Hotel. They had engineering, medical, and Sharia departments, and also a veterinary school, and they had more Islamic courses than Kabul University did. Fights would break out between the students of the two universities. The students of Dawa'a al-Jihad thought that the students at Kabul University were Communists, and we thought that they were fucking jihadis who had destroyed our country."

I had met Sayyaf for the first time a little more than a week before the parade, in his headquarters in Paghman. We sat on a red carpet under a walnut tree on a grassy, terraced hillside. He had a couple of friends with him, and a dozen or so armed bodyguards stood a short distance away. The view was pastoral and majestic. Tilled land dropped away into a patchwork of earth-colored hamlets, and in the distance stony, brown mountains fronted a long, jagged range of blue mountains capped with white snow.

King Zahir Shah had returned to Afghanistan that morning, and Sayyaf was dismissive about the whole thing. "Afghanistan, you know, is a destroyed country," he said, "and it needs strong and able people to rebuild it. But as far as I know, the king needs help from two people just to stand up. He's an old man." Sayyaf said that Karzai had a good chance of being ratified by the Loya Jirga, and he also tossed out the names of Fahim and Yunis Qanouni as possible leaders: the Panjshiris.

I told Sayyaf that I had been in Jalalabad in 1989, when the mujahideen—among them hundreds of Arab Wahhabi fighters recruited by Sayyaf—had laid siege to the city. He asked me why I had not come to his camp, which was off the road leading to Jalalabad from the Pakistani border, in the Khyber Pass. I didn't remind him that in those days his virulently anti-Western views had made him off-limits to most foreign journalists, many of whom had been terrorized by his Wahhabi friends. I just said that I had not had very good contacts. He nodded.

When I got up to leave, I saw a group of men walking toward me. One of them, who was surrounded by gunmen, was then-General Fahim's brother.

The day after the parade, I met Sayyaf at his house in the northwestern suburbs of Kabul, in a neighborhood that had been devastated in the fighting between his men and the Hazaras in the mid-nineties. Sayyaf was in a meeting in an upstairs room, and as it broke up I saw that one of the men with him was a mujahideen commander whose forces had helped take Kunduz from the Taliban in November. Sayyaf introduced him to me as the new governor of Kabul Province. When the other men left, we sat in the living room and he talked about himself. His father died when he was six, and he attended a madrasah in Paghman, and then the University of Kabul, where Burhanuddin Rabbani had been his teacher. Sayyaf was lecturing in Islamic studies in 1973, when Daoud overthrew the king and the Communists began to take over the government. He was in prison for nearly six years because of his Islamist activities, and then in exile in Pakistan. He claimed that he had spent most of the war years in Afghanistan, which gave him more legitimacy as a leader than some others had. And he said that he had been unjustly accused of being abusive: "Islam taught me to be kind to people."

After I had seen Sayyaf a few times, he became unavailable. He was ill or busy or I should call back tomorrow. And then the phone was switched off. So one hot Sunday morning in the middle of May I drove up to Paghman with one of Sayyaf's Ittihad fighters, a number of whom are bivouacked at a villa he owns in the Wazir Akbar Khan neighborhood in Kabul. It would have been difficult to get anywhere near Sayyaf without one of his men as an escort. The road between Paghman and Kabul is considered unsafe by late afternoon; several armed robberies and murders have occurred along it in recent months.

We stopped at a junction in the track where there was a sentry hut and a dozen or so fighters. I gave one of them my business card with a note scribbled on the back of it, addressed to Sayyaf, and the man took it and walked off toward an orchard a hundred metres or so in front of us. He came back in a few minutes and motioned us to drive on. Sayyaf was seated with several other men under the walnut tree where we had had our first conversation. One of the men was General Bismillah Khan, the Northern Alliance commander who had escorted the Arab assassins on excursions to the front lines when they were in the Panjshir Valley in August, posing as journalists. Bismillah Khan is now in charge of Kabul's military defenses.

I apologized for my intrusion, and said it was good that both Sayyaf and Bismillah Khan were there, since I wished to talk to them both. "As I am sure you know," I said to Sayyaf, "there are those who have expressed doubts about your relationship with Massoud's assassins, because they first came into the Northern Alliance territory through

you." Sayyaf's eyes narrowed, and he stared hard at me.
He translated what I had said to Bismillah Khan, who
speaks no English, and then he turned and said to me, in
English that seemed much more halting than during our
previous meetings, that they had let the Arabs in so that
they could see that they were good Muslims, and that their
forces had not been tainted by Westerners.

Bismillah Khan began speaking in Persian, and Sayyaf
translated. Khan said that in retrospect the two Arabs
behaved suspiciously, but he had not noticed this at the
time. "Now, when I think about them, I remember that
they had had beards but had recently shaved them off.
The marks of the beards were still there." He moved his
hands along his jawline to show what he meant. Sayyaf
chuckled and said that the Arabs had been very nervous
whenever they were in a car. "If they went with our people
to the bunkers"—at the Shamali front line—"they would
say, 'Please go slowly, because of our cameras; we don't
want them to be damaged.' Before the car moved, they
always put the cameras on their knees and told the driver
to be careful."

I asked Sayyaf how the two Arabs had come to be
with him in the first place. He described the phone call
from the former jihadi—"an Arab from Egypt, Abu Hani"—
who said he was in Bosnia and wanted Sayyaf to help the
two journalists get an interview with Massoud. Sayyaf also
described a meeting of most of the Northern Alliance leadership that took place in the Panjshir Valley while the
Arabs were there. He said that the Arabs had tried to
come into the meeting room but had been stopped by
guards. "They wanted to carry out their plan there," he
said. "They wanted to eliminate all the leaders of the resistance." Bismillah Khan said something in Persian, and

Sayyaf translated it as a comment about Sayyaf telling Massoud and Bismillah Khan that he had doubts about the Arabs and warning Massoud not to see them. Sayyaf threw up his hands to indicate that he had done all he could.

My final meeting with Sayyaf took place three days later, in another of his houses, off the road leading from Kabul to Paghman. He wasn't there when I arrived, but he soon drove up, in a convoy of Land Cruisers full of armed men. We sat in the living room with several aides and a general from Paktia Province who was visiting. I asked Sayyaf to describe his vision of the future of Afghanistan, and he spoke about the importance of an Islamic state, and about closely following the teachings of the Koran and not trying to introduce new ideas—the fundamentalist line. Then he brought up the betrayal of Afghanistan by the West in the early nineties, after the Soviets had retreated. "Once the Afghans kicked out the Red Army, the Western countries cut their backing," he said. "They had been supporting us only for their own interests."

I asked him about Osama bin Laden and the other Arabs whom he had known well and who had fought alongside him against the Russians. Osama had regarded Sayyaf as a father figure, had he not? Sayyaf smiled, and took off his turban and placed it on the sofa next to him. His hands were trembling. "I want to tell you frankly about those who became extremists," he said. "No one can name one example of harm done by those men when they were with us in the jihad. We were not extremists, and neither were they. But later, when Osama and his friends were brought to help the Taliban, who were extremists, they began to harm the world. I want to ask you, who brought Osama?"

Sayyaf was agitated. He sat on the edge of the sofa and leaned forward. He was expressing a conspiracy theory that is not uncommon in Kabul, even among reasonably sophisticated Afghans who have visited the West: that the Americans, with the aid of Pakistan, supported the Taliban and Osama bin Laden so that they could justify an invasion and take over the country. "The extremists backed by the foreigners were able to attack us," Sayyaf said. "We were the victims." His aides and the general from Paktia nodded in agreement. "I know that Osama and the Taliban did the assassination," Sayyaf said. "But who was behind them? All of those who were trying to help the Taliban were behind the assassination."

ABDULLAH ABDULLAH, the foreign minister of Afghanistan, is a sophisticated man with a great deal of charm, and he was a familiar figure on Western television as a spokesman for the Northern Alliance during the American bombing campaign that led to the defeat of the Taliban. I met him in a sitting room in his office in Kabul. The room had a blue carpet and plush blue chairs. There was a vase of freshly cut carnations on a side table. Abdullah was one of Massoud's best friends. "I was with him since 1985, during victories and defeats and the withdrawal from Kabul. I was ready to die for him ten times," he said. "He was extremely important for our country. He was exceptional. He was so humble, and so alive—the most alive creature I've ever met."

Abdullah was in New Delhi when Massoud was assassinated, and he was one of the few people who were told that Massoud had died. "When I heard the news," he said,

"I was one hundred percent certain that the United Front"—
the official name of the Northern Alliance—"would collapse. There was no doubt in my mind. I'm sure we would
have failed if the news had not been withheld." On September 11, Abdullah was trying to get back into Afghanistan.
"I heard the news on the BBC," he said. "I was trying to
focus on what was happening when the second plane hit.
And then I thought, It's Al Qaeda. I had said to U.S. officials
that Al Qaeda would intensify their work against the resistance." Abdullah dismisses the idea that the assassins
knew in advance about the attack on the World Trade Center and were trying to kill Massoud before it occurred.
"Osama bin Laden wouldn't have risked that," he said.
"What if they had been caught? But maybe they were given
a target date" for their part of the work.

Abdullah is skeptical also about Sayyaf's involvement
in the plot to kill Massoud. "I, personally, don't believe it,"
he said. Sayyaf made it possible for the Arabs to get to
Massoud, but this could have been justified if they had
been legitimate. "They behaved like journalists," Abdullah
said, "although when I went to see them they were very
rude." This was at the meeting of Northern Alliance leaders in the Panjshir that took place when the assassins were
Sayyaf's guests. "I introduced myself and they gave me a
look of hatred. I blame myself for not having picked up on
that." There had been other attempts on Massoud's life, and
in the end this one succeeded because of the kind of man
Massoud was. He tried to accommodate people. "Commander Massoud was a careless person," Abdullah said. "He
took some security measures, but he liked to be alone in
those interviews. And he never could have had one hundred percent security. We should have been able to iden-

tify the risk when those guys stayed in our area for three weeks. But we didn't."

YAHYA MASSOUD, THE ELDEST of Ahmed Shah Massoud's full brothers—he is fifty-two—took me on an overnight trip to the family's hometown of Bazarak, in the Panjshir Valley, three hours northeast of Kabul. Bazarak was Massoud's base during the jihad against the Soviets, and it is where his body is buried. Ahmed Shah Massoud was the second of the four brothers. Wali is the youngest. The other brother, Ahmed Zia, is now Afghanistan's ambassador to Moscow. Their father, an Afghan military officer who was killed in a car accident in 1993, had three wives. There are two more sons from the other marriages, and there are several sisters, although, as is customary in Afghanistan, Yahya didn't mention them. Yahya has been living in Warsaw for the last few years, where he was the first secretary at the Afghan embassy. He has a wife and six children in Switzerland. He doesn't plan to bring them back to Afghanistan, although he is living in Kabul for the time being, helping Wali organize the new Massoudist party.

Abdul Wadoud, a handsome, fair-skinned young man who is the son of one of Massoud's sisters, drove Yahya's luxurious Toyota Land Cruiser. Their other guest was an old family friend, Nur Sultan, an architect who was visiting Kabul after a fourteen-year exile in Reading, England. We travelled north across the Shamali plain. The Taliban methodically destroyed the Shamali after they seized power in Kabul, in order to create a no-man's-land between the capital and Massoud's front line, near the north end of the plain. It is now a vast mud Chernobyl of roofless and crumbling adobe farmhouses, collapsed walls, and barren fields. Many of the fields and roadsides are still planted with land mines, and here and there, uniformed de-miners wearing protective armor and safety helmets with transparent visors kneel or crouch, their faces close to the ground.

When we crossed the old front line, the landscape was suddenly transformed into a green arcadia. The farmhouses were intact, the orchards tended, and the vineyards bursting with new leaves. People walked and bicycled along the roadside, and mountain water burbled in irrigation ditches. The Taliban had once or twice pushed beyond this point, but never held the territory long enough to destroy it.

At the little market town of Charikar, we stopped to have lunch with General Bismillah Khan. Sofas and chairs had been placed in a large circle on the lawn, and Khan sat in the head chair and engaged his guests in conversation. After about a half hour or so of this, a jeep pulled up and men ran across the lawn toward us with large trays and bowls containing towers of white ice cream. We ate the ice cream, and then drove by convoy down a dirt road that led along an irrigation canal built in the sixties by the Chinese, and into a farmstead, where a group of men in turbans waited. Carpets were laid out under the trees around a pond. A bird cage with a white parakeet in it hung from one of the trees. Tea and bowls of *kishmish*—almonds and raisins and sweets—were served, and then we all filed into a long L-shaped room, where we were shown to our places on cushions placed around the walls. The entire floor was covered in tablecloths upon which was arrayed a feast of Afghan dishes: bowls of salad, rice pilaf with raisins and almonds, mutton, yogurt, soup, fruit, chicken and lamb, and basins full of tiny broiled quail, cooked whole.

There must have been five hundred of them. The little blackened cadavers rested in piles of scorched wings and feet and skulls and beaks and sunken eye sockets. Taking my cue from the men around me, I popped one in my mouth, and began crunching. I found that after four or five vigorous jaw movements, it was possible to swallow the thing and be done with the experience.

After the feast, Bismillah Khan and his entourage returned to Kabul, and we journeyed on into the Panjshir, which is really more of a canyon than a valley. A single narrow dirt road snakes alongside the Panjshir River, which runs between high mountains of gray and black scree and rock. At the mouth of the river, we drove through the small town of Gulbahar, where the two Arab terrorists had stayed, in one of the Northern Alliance's guest houses, after they crossed over from Taliban territory and were received by Abdul Rasul Sayyaf. Just outside town, Yahya pointed to a clutch of stone and brick buildings in the canyon wall, and said: "That was where Mr. Sayyaf lived." He said that his brother had accommodated Sayyaf and his several hundred fighters in that spot after Kabul fell to the Taliban.

In a couple of hours, we reached the promontory above Bazarak where Massoud is buried. Abdul Wadoud drove the Land Cruiser up a newly bulldozed road on the knoll and parked. We all got out and trooped over to a kind of dug-out-cave recess in the summit of the hill. It was surrounded by a brick wall with open arched windows and had a plastic-and-tin roof that was supported by stripped saplings and spiked with green flags with Koranic sayings on them. The tomb, a long dirt mound, was covered with a burgundy cloth with gold brocade decorations. Yahya and Abdul stood there, silently cupping their hands in prayer, with their eyes closed. Their friend, Nur Sultan, was over-

Yahya Massoud at his brother's tomb, near Bazarak

come by grief. He fell on his knees at the base of the tomb, weeping silently, gasping now and then in a strangled way for breath.

Nur Sultan stayed at the tomb for about half an hour, and then we took refuge from the rain in a nearby building, and Yahya introduced me to a man he described as the engineer in charge of turning Massoud's tomb into a proper mausoleum complex and pilgrimage site. He pulled out some blueprints and pointed to a ditch that ran along the scree all the way from Bazarak, about a mile distant. Soon, he said, it would carry water to this barren hilltop; the idea was that it would become a green parkland, planted with trees and flowers. The present, temporary tomb site would become a proper domed mausoleum, and Massoud's old headquarters, a yellow painted stone building that stood nearby, would be transformed into a Massoud museum. "We've kept everything exactly as it was when he was alive," Yahya said, "we haven't even moved a chair or desk." He said that there would be a library: "He had many books—over three thousand—and the museum will have his uniforms, his guns, and such things. It's a big project," Yahya said, looking around at the dismal hilltop.

A few hundred meters outside Bazarak, the road drops down the mountainside toward the river. The Massoud family compound, a hamlet-sized collection of flat-roofed adobe compounds, is on a steep slope overlooking the water. We drove up to a sentry hut, past a modern, white-painted cement house that Yahya said belonged to one of his sisters, who lives in Holland. The young soldier at the hut saluted and lowered the rope barrier, and we drove up the muddy track and parked alongside Massoud's grandfather's house. A smaller whitewashed building attached to it had belonged to his father and was where Ahmed Shah

Massoud was born. For a period during the jihad, Yahya said, Massoud had lived here and used part of the house as his command post.

A big rock wall topped with tin had been built into the steep hillside above their father's house. The wall formed a shining semicircle against the dark scree of the barren hill, enclosing a swath of terraced gardens that led to a modern, white house. Six or seven torrents of water arced gracefully down the hill from the house, bouncing from one terrace to another, and a stone pathway led up through a series of orange-colored latticed arbors. "This was the home Massoud was building for his family," said Yahya. "It was almost finished when he died." His wife and six children live in Iran now.

The house was a simple two-story structure made of concrete, but it had lots of windows and a glorious southern exposure. You could look down to Massoud's grandfather's house and to the curving river and the mountains beyond. The cement veranda surrounding the house had a snow-fed swimming pool, and a half-built sauna was set against the mountainside. Behind the house, a small canal was spanned by small bridges that led into an impressively stone-worked wall with several doorways. Yahya explained that Massoud had built a network of fortified cave rooms for his family in case their home was subjected to an aerial attack. On the next terrace down, there was a lawn and swings and a slide for Massoud's children, and farther down, a large orchard of almond, mulberry, apricot, and apple trees.

We walked back down along a pathway that led past the orchard and went into Massoud's father's house. It had recently been modernized, and the interior walls were painted a pale peach color. A single portrait hung on the wall. It was a pencil drawing of Massoud, smiling. That night, we slept on velveteen sleeping pads that had been placed for us in the room where Massoud was born.

A FEW DAYS LATER, in Kabul, I met Yahya at a Massoud family house in the Wazir Akbar Khan neighborhood, where he introduced me to Commander Aziz Majrou, one of Ahmed Shah Massoud's oldest and most loyal mujahideen officers. Aziz had been badly wounded in the war against the Soviets. His left hand was scarred and missing a thumb and he limped. "Majrou means 'wounded person,'" he explained to me, shyly.

Aziz had met Massoud in 1978, when the first of Afghanistan's Marxist leaders, Taraki, was in power. Aziz was a twenty-year-old mechanic and Massoud was one of the emerging Islamist leaders who were trying to organize guerrilla insurgencies. He wrote a letter to the people in Aziz's village, Dasht-i-Debat, in the Panjshir Valley. "The elders gathered the men of the village in a secret place and read out the letter," Aziz recalled. "It said that there was a Communist regime in Afghanistan that wanted to change our culture and that we must defend ourselves." The letter was a summons to holy war. Aziz said that he and a hundred or so other men from the village began to organize themselves, although only a few of them had guns or fighting experience. The elders in Safichir, a nearby village, had also received a letter from Massoud, and men there began to organize also, and to wait for Massoud to come to them. "About a month after the letter came," Aziz said, "Massoud arrived, and then a third village, Paian, joined us. These were the first three villages in the Panjshir to organize."

Massoud came with about twenty men, including several relatives and friends. "I thought that he was going to be a big man, with a big beard and a turban," Aziz said. "Someone maybe in his forties or fifties. But he was almost the youngest man in the group." Massoud would have been about twenty-six years old then. "He was an honest man," Aziz recalled. "He didn't seem to be interested in money, and he acted like a leader." Aziz stayed with Massoud until he was assassinated. His duties changed over the years, especially after he was injured, but he remained a mujahideen. At the end, he said, he had worked as a deputy division commander in the Panjshir.

I asked Aziz who he thought had killed Massoud. "There is no doubt it was the terrorists," he said, the Taliban and Pakistan. "But, unfortunately, most of the provincial commanders in the Panjshir did not pay enough attention to the dangers he faced. His security was not very well organized. We had warned him to be careful."

Were the assassins able to kill Massoud because of the negligence of his officers? I asked Aziz. Or was there a betrayal from within the Northern Alliance?

"Sayyaf is, of course, very suspicious," Aziz replied. "Perhaps he knew of the plan. Or perhaps he didn't know what the terrorists were up to and was used by them."

I MET BISMILLAH KHAN again in late May, at his base in Kabul. He shared it with a Swedish contingent of the I.S.A.F. He has an office on the rooftop of a building that has a rose garden and a lawn and a huge, sixties-style swimming pool. The Swedes were giving a Taste of Sweden barbecue when I arrived, and Bismillah Khan and his men were lined up with paper plates and plastic utensils to get their food. They were obviously ill at ease, and not a little offended, since at an Afghan feast a guest sits and is served.

Some of the Afghans didn't know how to eat with forks and knives, and those who did helped them. They whispered about what was on their plates: barbecued beef, chicken, potatoes, and bamboo shoots. They didn't know what bamboo was, and most of them didn't touch it. They had never eaten potatoes with the skins on. A few of the men cracked jokes in Dari about the meat, which they thought might be dog, or pork. Others said that it wasn't *halal,* that is, that a butcher had not uttered "God is great!" when the animal's throat was cut.

At the end of the meal, the Swedish chef announced that he wanted to wish one of the other soldiers happy birthday, and, as was the custom in Sweden, he would present him with a gift. This was all translated to the Afghans, who were puzzled, since they don't celebrate birthdays. The chef unwrapped a bottle of whiskey and handed it to the soldier. "And now," the chef said, "our friend must share his gift, as is the custom in Afghanistan, with everyone here. It will take, I estimate, five minutes." And he laughed at his joke.

Two of Bismillah Khan's aides ran over to the Swede's translator and pointed out that this was a big mistake. Fridoun, my translator, muttered, "Don't they learn anything at all about Afghan culture before they come?" The whiskey bottle was removed, and Bismillah Khan, who had politely eaten everything on his plate during dinner, rose and thanked his hosts and shook the officers' hands.

Later, in Bismillah Khan's office, I asked him about one of the key elements in Sayyaf's explanation of his role in the matter of Massoud's assassination. Sayyaf had told me, and others, that he had warned Bismillah Khan and

Massoud that the Arabs might be dangerous and that he didn't trust them. Bismillah Khan said only that Sayyaf had told Massoud that the Arabs seemed "strange." He became testy when pressed and said that I should talk to Sayyaf. He also said that he hadn't sent a car to pick up the Arabs. They had been picked up by Sayyaf's men. "Who brought them from the front line to Kabul?" I asked.

"I don't know," Bismillah Khan said. "Maybe the Taliban."

The Arab assassins had been taken to Sayyaf's house and given tea, and were introduced to a man named Qazi Karamatullah Siddiq, who spoke Arabic and was assigned to accompany them while they were in the Panjshir. Siddiq is a Muslim scholar and a graduate in Sharia law from Dawa'a al-Jihad, Sayyaf's university near Peshawar. He now works in one of the ministries in the interim government, and I talked with him about the Arabs. Although Siddiq is a Sayyaf loyalist, he contradicted several of Sayyaf's recollections, most notably the one about the assassins almost getting into the meeting of Northern Alliance leaders in the Panjshir, supposedly to kill them all. This was a story that I had heard repeatedly as evidence that Sayyaf was not involved in the plot to kill Massoud, since he would have been killed himself. But Siddiq says that the Arabs never got near the meeting, because Sayyaf had refused, in advance, to give them permission. He says that Sayyaf then arranged for the Arabs to interview Massoud in Khoja Bahauddin. Siddiq also said that Sayyaf never mentioned any suspicions about the Arabs until after the assassination, although Siddiq didn't seem to think this implicated Sayyaf. "Professor Sayyaf and Ahmed Shah Massoud were like brothers," Siddiq assured me. "No one was more sad than Professor Sayyaf when Massoud died."

Conspiracy theories are given credence in Afghanistan not least because there have been, historically, a lot of conspiracies. The reigning political ethos is survival of the fittest, and alliances are fluid. Afghans are geographically isolated, xenophobic, and cynical from years of war. Sayyaf helped the assassins, and most of the people I spoke to who were close to Massoud—relatives, intelligence agents, military commanders—believe that he must have had some sense, if not explicit knowledge, of the assassins' plans. But he was only one—perhaps the final—link in a chain of people who made it possible for the two Arabs to get to Khoja Bahauddin with their sophisticated explosives and well-choreographed suicide plan. For instance, among the CDs and notebooks and verses from the Koran found in the Arabs' things after the assassination was a letter of recommendation written by the head of the Afghan Red Crescent Society (shocking documentation of the culture of complicity and appeasement that had developed between NGOs and the Taliban). Massoud's assassins were linked to Osama bin Laden and Al Qaeda and, by inference, to the World Trade Center bombing. "These links are so strong," an Afghan intelligence agent close to the investigation of Massoud's death said to me, "that they leave no doubt to anyone in intelligence, with knowledge of terrorist organizations, and of Afghanistan, that the two events were connected."

One afternoon toward the end of May, I went to lunch at Wali Massoud's house. He had several guests, including a group of Afghan-American businessmen. One of them, who lives in Virginia and works for DynCorp, an American defense contractor, told me that he had been away for twenty-five years but was thinking of returning if he could do some business for his company.

Wali and I were able to talk for a few minutes in a corner, and I said to him that an Afghan intelligence officer had told me that, although several European intelligence agencies are investigating his brother's murder, there isn't much of an investigation taking place in Afghanistan.

"That's right," he said. "There is no investigation here at all."

I asked Wali if people were preoccupied by the intense preparations for the Loya Jirga. I had been struck by the fact that Sayyaf seemed to be very involved in the deal making that was going on. Why would so many of those who revered Massoud be prepared to cut deals with a man who is suspected of betraying him?

"All of these people," Wali said, "are involved in politics."

Abdul Rasul Sayyaf, center, at his headquarters in Paghman.
General Bismillah Khan is on the far right.

Afghan Defense Minister Fahim at a parade in Kabul on April 28, 2002, to com-
memorate the tenth anniversary of the mujahideen's entry into the city and their
victory over the Soviets. Photographs of Massoud and Hamid Karzai, who was then
the interim prime minister of Afghanistan, are taped to the windshield of his jeep.

Interior Minister Yunis Qanouni and Foreign Minister Abdullah Abdullah at the Kabul airport a few weeks before the Loya Jirga, which was convened on June 11, 2002

Afterword

A t the Loya Jirga, which was held shortly after I left Afghanistan, King Zahir Shah took himself out of the running and endorsed Hamid Karzai, whose tenure as Afghanistan's head of state was extended for eighteen months. Burhanuddin Rabbani, who had been unable to muster enough support for his own candidacy, also backed Karzai. Two of the "Three Panjshiris," Abdullah Abdullah and Marshal Fahim, kept their jobs, as foreign minister and defense minister, respectively. Fahim also became one of Karzai's three vice presidents, along with Karim Khalili, a Shia Hazara warlord, and the Pashtun strongman of Jalalabad, Haji Abdul Qadir, although Haji Qadir was in office less than a month. He was assassinated early in July. The third Panjshiri, Yunis Qanouni, resigned as interior minister so that Karzai could appoint a Pashtun to that position. Qanouni reluctantly accepted the education ministry and an additional role as one of Karzai's national security advisers. Wali Massoud, who had hoped to obtain some sort of senior position for himself, left the Loya Jirga empty-handed.

Abdul Rasul Sayyaf was a prominent figure at the Loya Jirga. He argued that the country should remain an Islamic state. (Under President Rabbani, Afghanistan became the Islamic State of Afghanistan, which the Taliban renamed the Islamic Emirate of Afghanistan.) An eloquent retort to that argument was delivered by none other than Gul Agha Shirzai, the governor of Kandahar, who pointed out that the term "Islamic" had been degraded by the abuses of past Afghan leaders. In the end, the new government was called the Afghanistan Transitional Islamic State."

The Loya Jirga was a disappointment to many delegates who had hoped, perhaps unrealistically, that it would be a real exercise in representative democracy. In spite of Karzai's promise to stamp out "warlordism," the position of strongmen from the old Northern Alliance was, if anything, strengthened, and secular reformers lost ground. The outspoken women's affairs minister, Seema Samar, was branded "Afghanistan's Salman Rushdie," and she lost her job. But for all its flaws, the Loya Jirga represented an extraordinary moment in modern Afghanistan, the closest thing to an open political debate most Afghans had ever experienced. Certainly, none of them could have dreamed of such an event taking place a year earlier.

Professor Muhammad Kazem Ahung, the despondent former dean of journalism at Kabul University, whom I had interviewed for the "City of Dreams" piece, was reinstated by the university and selected as one of nine members of the Loya Jirga commission, a great honor. When I visited him at his newly recarpeted home not long before I left Afghanistan, he said, smiling, "At my age, and after all of these years sitting here, useless, I have an opportunity to serve my country! I cannot tell you how happy, how proud, I am. My life has begun over, I have been reborn."

Mamur Hassan, the warlord of Dasht-i-Qala, was said to be in good health and still living with his wives and children in his hometown, which is no longer a frontline position in a war zone, just a little trading settlement by a river near the Tajik border. I heard that Bashir, the Taliban prisoner who was being kept in a hole by another warlord near Dasht-i-Qala, was executed in November, after the Taliban defenses in northern Afghanistan crumbled and the Northern Alliance marched on Taloqan. It was a plausible story.

At last word, Idris, the irrepressible aetheist of Faizabad, had found a good-paying job as a translator for a Western relief organization, and had gained a considerable amount of weight. Walid, the ascerbic young Tajik who was close to Rabbani's court, was also still in Faizabad, but hoping to travel to the United States. He was applying for a scholarship that had been made available to Afghans.

Fridoun, the affable medical student who first guided me around the ruins of Kabul, and who also worked with me as a translator, went back to Kabul University to take his medical school exams. Qias, the young translator who loyally accompanied Thomas Dworzak and me from Kabul to Tora Bora and on to Kandahar—and who also worked with us when we returned to Kabul—took over our rented house on Flower Street and planned to run it as a guest house for foreign journalists.

Massoud's tomb was completed in time for the first anniversary of his death. It is a small, graceful-looking, round building, painted white, with a green dome. On September seventh, two days after an assassin in Kandahar almost killed him, Hamid Karzai went to Bazarak to pay his respects to Massoud. On the ninth, a national day of mourning, thousands of Afghans gathered around the tomb, standing vigil in the sharp autumn light of the Panjshir Valley.

Glossary of Names

Abdullah Abdullah: One of Ahmed Shah Massoud's closest aides. He was the foreign minister of the Northern Alliance, and after the fall of the Taliban he became the Afghan foreign minister. Abdullah Abdullah is one of the "Three Panjshiris," along with Muhammad Fahim and Yunis Qanouni.

Professor Muhammad Kazem Ahung: A veteran Afghan journalist, newspaper editor, and author, Ahung was the dean of journalism at Kabul University until his ouster by the Taliban.

Hafizullah Amin: Served as prime minister for Afghanistan's first Marxist president, Nur Muhammad Taraki, whom he overthrew in September 1979 and had executed a month later. Amin's own presidency lasted only three months. In December 1979, he was assassinated, reportedly by Soviet commandos. Moscow installed a more pliant Marxist, Babrak Karmal, as president, and sent the Red Army into Afghanistan.

Engineer Muhammad Aref: Headed Massoud's security services. Massoud was assassinated in his office in Khoja Bahauddin. Aref was out of the room when the bomb went off.

Muhammad Daoud: A strong Afghan nationalist and modernizer, Daoud abolished the monarchy and declared Afghanistan a republic in July 1973 after toppling his cousin, King Zahir Shah. President Daoud's regime was left-leaning and firmly anti-Islamist, which gave rise to the mujahideen guerrilla movements. Eventually, Daoud alienated the leftists. In April 1978, he and most of his immediate family were killed during the so-called Saur Revolt, after which the Marxist politician Nur Muhammad Taraki took power.

Fahim Dashty: A young Afghan journalist, and protégé of Massoud, Dashty founded Ariana Films, a documentary company that chronicled Massoud's exploits. He was standing behind the suicidal assassin when Massoud was killed, and he was badly wounded. After the ouster of the Taliban, Dashty became the editor of the *Kabul Weekly,* a newspaper published in English, Farsi, and Pashto.

Abdul Rashid Dostum: An Uzbek warlord from northern Afghanistan, whose kaleidoscopic political alliances and penchant for battlefield butchery earned him an unsavory reputation. He was a Soviet ally in the nineteen-eighties but switched sides in 1992, joining forces with Massoud and helping to bring about the fall of Afghanistan's last Communist president, Najibullah, and the mujahideen seizure of Kabul. Dostum joined Massoud and President Rabbani in Kabul, helping to defend it against their archrival, Gulbuddin Hekmatyar. But he double-crossed them and joined forces with Hekmatyar in 1994. In 1996, as the Taliban marched on Kabul, Dostum rejoined Massoud. The following year, when the Taliban were advancing in the north, he fled to Turkey, then returned to the fray, and in

1998 he fled the country again. In the spring of 2001, Dostum agreed to fight alongside the Northern Alliance. Assisted by a group of U.S. Special Forces commandos, Dostum seized the northern city of Mazar-i-Sharif in November 2001. His forces are believed to have massacred hundreds of Taliban, Pakistani, and Al Qaeda fighters there, as well as after the fall of Kunduz. Dostum's men also quelled the prison uprising in which nearly two hundred prisoners, as well as an American CIA agent, died, and where the "American Taliban," John Walker Lindh, was captured. Dostum became Hamid Karzai's deputy defense minister.

Muhammad Qasim Fahim: The most powerful of the "Three Panjshiris." He served as deputy commander of the Northern Alliance until Massoud's assassination, when he assumed the military leadership of the anti-Taliban movement. General Fahim became Afghanistan's defense minister under Hamid Karzai.

Abdul Haq: Gained prominence as a mujahideen leader during the anti-Soviet jihad of the nineteen-eighties. He was from a prominent Pashtun clan in eastern Afghanistan, and was an early critic of the Arab extremists who were invited to join the fighting by warlords like Gulbuddin Hekmatyar and Adbul Rasul Sayyaf. After the Taliban took power, Haq became a businessman in the United Arab Emiretes. In October 2001, he was wooed back to Afghanistan by the CIA, who saw him as a potential post-Taliban leader. They airdropped him into southern Afghanistan, where he was quickly run to ground and summarily hung by the Taliban. It was after Haq's death that Washington tapped Hamid Karzai as the man to lead Afghanistan. One of Haq's brothers, Haji Qadir, was made a vice president in Karzai's government at the Loya Jirga and was assassinated in July 2002.

Mamur Hassan: Amiable Uzbek warlord who commanded the frontline anti-Taliban defenses for the Northern Alliance from his hometown, Dasht-i-Qala.

Gulbuddin Hekmatyar: A vehemently anti-Western Islamist, Hekmatyar fled the country after the Daoud coup in 1973. Originally a protégé, together with Massoud, of Burhanuddin Rabbani, Hekmatyar broke with them and formed his own mujahideen party, the Hezb-i-Islami, which became the favored Afghan faction of Pakistan's intelligence service, the I.S.I. Hekmatyar received the lion's share of the covert CIA aid that was channelled to the mujahideen through the I.S.I. during the jihad against the Soviets. After Rabbani became president of Afghanistan in 1992, Hekmatyar refused to assume his post of prime minister, and besieged Kabul from the surrounding hills. Thousands of civilians were killed in Hekmatyar's rocket attacks. In 1996, having been abandoned by his I.S.I. sponsors in favor of the advancing Taliban, Hekmatyar finally joined the Rabbani-Massoud government and pushed through a series of stringent Islamic Sharia laws. But Kabul soon fell to the Taliban, and Rabbani and Massoud fled to the north. Hekmatyar made his way to Iran, where he remained during the Taliban's tenure. In the autumn of 2001, he denounced the American bombing campaign and urged Afghans to fight alongside the Taliban. In early 2002, he slipped back into Afghanistan to rally his loyalists against the American "puppet regime" of Hamid Karzai.

Idris (pseudonym): A former journalist who taught himself English, Idris is a resolutely anticlerical Afghan. I met him in Faizabad, where he worked intermittently as a translator. He is the author of the unpublished "The Crazy Dogs of Certain Centuries."

Jamshid: Massoud's nephew and brother-in-law. He was also Massoud's private secretary, and was with him when he was assassinated. Jamshid escaped death because he had left the room when Massoud's assassins detonated their bomb.

Babrak Karmal: The third Marxist ruler of Afghanistan, Karmal was installed by the Soviets after the assassination of Hafizullah Amin in December 1979. He remained in power until 1986, when he was ousted bloodlessly by his secret police chief, Muhammad Najibullah. He died of cancer in exile in Moscow in 1996.

Ahmed Wali Karzai: One of Hamid Karzai's younger brothers, and his personal representative in Kandahar.

Hamid Karzai: The telegenic and well-mannered scion of the prominent Pashtun Populzai clan, and a former deputy foreign minister in the Rabbani government, Karzai was chosen as the chairman of Afghanistan's interim government at a meeting of Afghan leaders held in Bonn in December 2001. He was elected president at the Loya Jirga in June 2002.

Massoud Khalili: A close personal friend of Ahmed Shah Massoud, Khalili served as the Northern Alliance's envoy to New Delhi. He was in Khoja Bahauddin to see Massoud in September 2001, and was in the room with Massoud when he was assassinated. Khalili's legs were badly burned and he received hundreds of pieces of shrapnel in the bomb explosion; he also lost the hearing in one ear and was blinded in one eye.

General Bismillah Khan: Commanded the Northern Alliance's front line on the Shamali plain, north of Kabul.

In August 2001, Khan unwittingly played host to Massoud's two Arab killers for several days, giving them an interview and even sending them to inspect his troops' positions. The night before Massoud was assassinated, Khan successfully fought off a concerted Taliban offensive. After the fall of the Taliban, he became the chief of military security for Kabul.

Ahmed Shah Massoud: The Lion of the Panjshir. Born in 1952 in the Panjshir Valley, the son of a military officer in King Zahir Shah's army, Massoud was raised in Kabul, where he attended the French-run Lycée Istiqlal, an elite private high school. He was an engineering student at Kabul University, where he became involved in the budding Islamist movement led by Burhanuddin Rabbani. Along with other young Islamists, he fled to Pakistan when Muhammad Daoud established a coalition government with Afghan Communist parties. As a member of Rabbani's Jamiat-i-Islami Party, Massoud took part in the first mujahideen attacks, a series of abortive raids carried out in 1975 against Afghan army posts. In 1978, following Daoud's overthrow by the Marxist leader Nur Muhammad Taraki, Massoud sneaked back into Afghanistan to recruit fighters for the mujahideen cause. After the Soviet invasion, the charismatic Massoud consolidated his position as the leading Jamiat military commander, based in the Panjshir Valley, where he earned a reputation as a brilliant battlefield tactician and strategist. In 1992, with the fall of President Najibullah, Massoud led the mujahideen seizure of Kabul and served as President Rabbani's defense minister. During the factional fighting in Kabul, sparked by Gulbuddin Hekmatyar (who over the years had become his archrival), Massoud led the defense of the city. In 1996, the Taliban forced him back to the Panjshir. For the next five years Massoud led the fight against the Taliban as the military commander of the Northern Alliance. In 2000, after the fall of his headquarters in the northern city of Taloqan, Massoud fell back to the little town of Khoja Bahauddin, on the Afghan border with Tajikistan. In 2001, in a bid to strengthen the anti-Taliban resistance, he began wooing back his old rivals, like Abdul Rashid Dostum, and he travelled to Europe for the first time in his life, where he appealed for Western assistance for what he described as Afghanistan's "war against terrorism." He was assassinated by two Arabs posing as journalists on September 9, 2001.

Ahmed Wali Massoud: The youngest of Ahmed Shah Massoud's full brothers. He lived and studied in England, where he earned a degree in public diplomacy and went to work at Afghanistan's embassy in London, eventually becoming the chargé d'affaires. He returned to Kabul after the Taliban collapse, and in the spring of 2002 he launched a new "Massoudist" political party called the National Movement of Afghanistan.

Yahya Massoud: The eldest Massoud brother. During the Taliban regime, Yahya worked as a diplomat at the Northern Alliance's embassy in Warsaw. He returned to Kabul in 2002.

Najibullah (Najib): Took power in Afghanistan in a bloodless coup in 1986, when he deposed the country's third Marxist ruler, Babrak Karmal. Najib, who had served as the head of KHAD, Afghanistan's feared Marxist-era secret police and intelligence organization, managed to survive in power after the Soviet military withdrawal was completed in 1989. He resigned in 1992, when attempts to negotiate a settlement with the mujahideen broke down. As the mujahideen swept into Kabul, Najib tried to flee by airplane but was thwarted. He took refuge in the United Nations compound in Kabul, where he lived for the next four years. In September 1996, when the Taliban entered the city, they broke into the compound, seized Najib and his brother, tortured them, castrated and shot them, and then hung their bodies in a downtown traffic circle.

Mullah Naquibullah (Naquib): The warlord of the Argandhab valley, north of Kandahar, and the leader of the Alokozai tribe. He fought alongside Massoud against the Soviets and their Afghan allies throughout the nineteen-eighties, and when the mujahideen seized power in 1992, Naquib became the supreme commander of Kandahar. In 1994 he turned the city over to the advancing Taliban militia. In the autumn of 2001, Hamid Karzai and his brother Wali contacted him and asked for his help in ousting the Taliban, but Mullah Naquib stayed on the fence until December, when the U.S. bombing campaign was well under way, at which point he negotiated a surrender agreement on behalf of the besieged Taliban leaders. There was no surrender, however, since during the night of December 6 the main Taliban leaders, including Mullah Omar, escaped. Naquib's fighters and those of Gul Agha Shirzai skirmished for control of the city, but, in a peace deal brokered by Karzai, Gul Agha was made governor of the province. Naquib, who was under suspicion of having helped Mullah Omar escape, was offered the lesser job as commander of Kandahar's military garrison. He refused the post, but handed it over to his deputy.

Yunis Qanouni: One of the powerful triumvirate of former Massoud deputies known as the "Three Panjshiris." Qanouni became Afghanistan's interior minister after the Northern Alliance seized Kabul in November 2001, and he retained his post during the six-month interim administration of Hamid Karzai. At the Loya Jirga, he was made education minister and Karzai's adviser on national security.

Burhanuddin Rabbani: The president of the Islamic State of Afghanistan after the mujahideen took power in Kabul in 1992, and then the nonmilitary head of the Northern Alliance, which was the only government recognized by most foreign powers when the Taliban were in control of the country. Rabbani was born in Faizabad, in northeastern Afghanistan. He studied at Al-Azhar University in Cairo and taught theology at Kabul University. One of the early leaders of Afghanistan's Islamist movement, he founded the Jamiat-i-Islami in 1971. He fled to Pakistan after Muhammad Daoud seized power, and in 1975 his followers, among them Ahmed Shah Massoud, launched a series of botched attacks against the Daoud government. Rabbani's party was one of the leading armed resistance factions in Afghanistan during the jihad against the Soviets in the nineteen-eighties. In November 2001, following the Taliban collapse, Rabbani returned to Kabul and reluctantly accepted Hamid Karzai as the head of the government.

Salahuddin Rabbani: The eldest of Burhanuddin Rabbani's ten children, Salahuddin lived in London until Massoud was assassinated, when he returned to northern Afghanistan to help his father.

Dr. Rostum (pseudonym): A medical doctor from the northern city of Taloqan, Rostum works for a Western relief organization in Faizabad.

Abdul Rasul Sayyaf: One of Afghanistan's leading Muslim fundamentalists. Like Burhanuddin Rabbani, who was once his teacher, Sayyaf studied theology at Kabul University and went on to earn a degree from Al-Azhar University in Cairo. He returned to Afghanistan, where he taught Islamic studies at Kabul University and was a founding member of Afghanistan's Islamist movement. He spent nearly six years in prison during the secular Daoud regime. After he was released in 1980, Sayyaf fled to Pakistan, where he quickly established himself as a leader of the anti-Communist mujahideen alliance based in the city of Peshawar. He formed the Ittihad-al-Islami (Islamic Union) in 1981, with backing from Saudi Arabia and conservative Arab groups. Sayyaf also founded a university called Dawa'a al-Jihad (Convert and Struggle) in an Afghan refugee camp near Peshawar. It became known as a terrorist training school. Sayyaf accepted hundreds of foreign jihadi volunteers, among them Osama bin Laden. When the mujahideen seized power in 1992, Sayyaf moved to Kabul and served as Rabbani's deputy in the short-lived coalition government. His forces played a key role in the factional fighting that destroyed much of Kabul, and they were accused by Human Rights Watch of atrocities. In 1996 Sayyaf fled the capital along with Massoud. In the fall of 2001, he permitted two Arab's posing as journalists to pass through Northern Alliance lines. The Arabs assassinated Massoud.

Muhammad Nazir Shafiee: A young foreign relations adviser to former president Rabbani. After the fall of the Taliban in November 2001, Nazir accompanied Rabbani to Kabul.

Yassir al-Sirri: An Egyptian Islamist who ran the London-based Islamic Observation Centre, which was devoted to disseminating extremist Muslim viewpoints, including those of Osama bin Laden and the Taliban. Al-Sirri was arrested in October 2001 on suspicion of helping the assassins who killed Massoud. A British judge ordered his release in May 2002.

Gul Agha Shirzai: The governor of Kandahar. Gul Agha was governor during Rabbani's presidency, while his rival, Mullah Naquib, was the province's supreme military commander. He was forced to flee to Pakistan when Naquib turned Kandahar over to the Taliban in 1994. On December 7, 2001, his army of fighters reentered the city of Kandahar and skirmished briefly with Mullah Naquib's forces, but Hamid Karzai interceded. Gul Agha was named to his old post as governor.

Nur Muhammad Taraki: The first Marxist leader of Afghanistan. A prominent Afghan author, editor, and journalist, Taraki was a founding member of Afghanistan's Communist Party in 1965 and helped lead the so-called Saur Revolt against Muhammad Daoud in April 1978. Taraki renamed the country the Democratic Republic of Afghanistan, instituting a regime of radical socialism. In September 1979, Taraki was overthrown by his prime minister, Hafizullah Amin, and secretly executed a month later.

Walid (pseudonym): A politically astute young Tajik man in Faizabad who was close to the inner circle of former President Burhanuddin Rabbani.

King Muhammad Zahir Shah: Became Afghanistan's king in 1933, at the age of nineteen, following the assassination of his father. Zahir Shah was politically moderate and reform-minded. He reigned until 1973, when he was overthrown by his cousin, Muhammad Daoud, who abolished the monarchy and declared a republic. Zahir Shah spent the next twenty-nine years in exile, in Rome. In April 2002 he returned to Kabul to assist in the process of national reconciliation.

Acknowledgments

I owe a lot of thanks, especially to my editor at *The New Yorker,* Sharon DeLano, for the considerable skills, insights, and sheer hard work that she put into my pieces, and into this book. To David Remnick—who knows what it takes to get the story—for his advice, his unstinting patience, and his faith. To Dorothy Wickenden and Pamela McCarthy, for helping to make it all happen, over and over again. To Andy Young, for his irrepressible good humor, enthusiasm, and considerable fact-checking skills, and to Liesl Schillinger and Nandi Rodrigo for helping to ensure that my more egregious errors never made it into print. Elisabeth Biondi, Meredith Blum, Daniel Cappello, Kevin Denges, Perri Dorset, Ann Goldstein, Risa Leibowitz, Jacob Lewis, Natasha Lunn, Francine Schore, and Hellyn Sher were indispensable allies in the teamwork that went into each of the Afghan pieces published in *The New Yorker.* Thanks, as always, to my publisher at Grove/Atlantic, Morgan Entrekin, and to Amy Hundley, Judy Hottensen, Charles Woods, and Muriel Jorgensen, and to Sarah Chalfant at the Wylie Agency.

A great many people helped me while I was travelling in the field. I am grateful to Liza Faktor, Noushin

Farzam, Nick Richards, and Abdul Latif Alemi. Special thanks to Qias, Fridoun, and Nabi, who proved to be not only capable translators, but honest and loyal friends. To John Weaver for his samaritanlike hospitality in Dasht-i-Qala. To Tyler Bridges, Robyn Dixon, Janine de Giovanni, Yuri Kosarev, Bob Nickelsberg, Heathcliffe "Mullah" O'Malley, Julius Strauss, Andrew Testa, and Iva Zimova for their comradeship. Thomas Dworzak was my companion and colleague the entire time I was in Afghanistan, and he made the experience bearable, and, quite often, an unexpected delight.

I am grateful to my friends in Colombia—Ricardo, José Luis, Mafer, Pedro, los dos Jaimes, Carlitos, Virginia and Pablo, La Diva Miriam, Mirta, Roberto, Rafa, Chila, and Julio—for reminding me during a crucial interlude that there is more to life than war, there is also Carnaval. And to Erica, Bella, Rosie, and Maximo, for understanding why I had to be away from home so much after September 11, and for putting up with me when I came back.

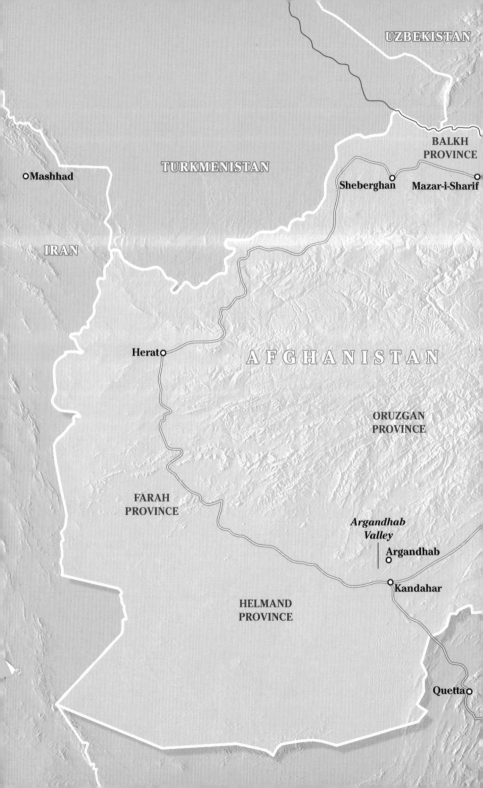